Cool News About Retail

Cool News About Retail

✳

From Warhol to Wal-Mart

Tim Manners

iUniverse, Inc.

New York Lincoln Shanghai

Cool News About Retail
From Warhol to Wal-Mart

iUniverse, Inc.

For information address:
iUniverse, Inc.
2021 Pine Lake Road, Suite 100
Lincoln, NE 68512
www.iuniverse.com

ISBN: 0-595-30641-1

Printed in the United States of America

For Holly and Spencer, my kids, and inveterate shoppers both.

Contents

Introduction

"The people who have the best fame," wrote Andy Warhol, "are those who have their name on stores. The people with very big stores named after them are the ones I'm really jealous of."

That was a quote from a *Cool News of the Day* item published on August 6, 2003, which would have been Andy Warhol's 75th birthday. It was one of many items published in our daily newsletter that had to do with retail. Regular *Cool News* readers know that retail is a favorite subject, precisely because so much of what happens at retail is just so cool.

We thought it would be cooler still to review all of the retail-centric *Cool News* stories we've published over the past year or so to see whether any patterns emerged. Sure enough, we spotted a few, and this collection is a reflection of what we caught.

What we noticed first was a cluster of stories about successful retailers. It should come as no surprise that Wal-Mart received some coverage here. An item entitled, "In Wal-Mart We Trust," derived from a *USA Today* article by Jim Hopkins published on January 29, 2003, provided a sobering summary of just how dominant Sam Walton's idea has become.

"Successes" also includes Sears, Circuit City, The Coffee Bean, Monro Muffler Brake, Tommy Bahama, CarMax, Whole Foods, Zingerman's Deli…and Wal-Mart de Mexico. Plenty of insights here, even for a relatively short section that begins and ends with Wal-Mart!

Coming up with a handle for our second cluster of stories was something of a struggle. In this part, we have stories about loyalty programs, customer service, shopper behavior, merchandising, technologies and pricing.

Ultimately, we decided to categorize these stories under the rubric of "Selling," because that's really the main point of these various vignettes. Some might find it intriguingly appropriate that the last two items—"Filene's Doghouse" and "Customer Rage Management"—are about selling gone awry.

Things become even more interesting in our next category, the one called "Concepts." This is where the creative juices really begin to flow, with stories about retailers who build their businesses not on the usual merchandising mix, but on the basis of a specific idea. Whether these retailers are successful is less important than that they are trying something new and different that appears to be pretty smart.

In "Saks for Tots," Saks Fifth Avenue decides to go up against Toys R Us and Wal-Mart by re-opening its toy department. Dylan's Candy Bar does double duty as a laboratory for Hershey and Mars—not to mention Target and Wal-Mart. A New York bar called Hi-Fi has patrons lined up to use its "Extra Large Digital Jukebox."

Stepping it up a notch, our fourth banner is called "Hybrids," and it includes examples of retailers who have cross-pollinated in some way, shape or form. Sometimes this entails a mixture of retail with another medium—such as *Surface*, which is both a hotel and a magazine. Or it is a combination of two types of retail—pairing supermarkets with restaurants; department stores with nightclubs; or art museums with fashion boutiques.

One can almost see Andy Warhol cracking a Mona Lisa smile at this confluence of art and commerce. After all, when he was envying retailers, he wasn't turning green over Wal-Mart!

This brings us to our last—and longest—section of our collection. It is called "Atmospherics" and it is our favorite cluster of *Cool News* stories.

Please note that we did not call this section, "Experiential," and for this we hope you are grateful. As we see it, experiential applies to any type of retail. For all its no-nonsense, stripped down, low-price merchandising, Wal-Mart is an experience, right?

Atmospherics, however is something else again.

The really cool thing is that atmospherics seems to manifest itself most often in places one might not necessarily think of as retail, first and foremost. Indeed, our stories are found in airplanes, movie theaters and bowling alleys. In "The Buyer's Club," retail is a sidewalk on New York's

Lower East Side. In the "The New Drive-Ins" it's in a cemetery. In "Phish and the Bunny" it's the Loring Air Force Base (actually, what used to be the Loring Air Force Base).

So, what are we to make of all of these stories? What we make of it is that retail is extraordinarily under-developed as an engine of sales and marketing. What makes it so special, in fact, is that retail is the only place where sales and marketing happen simultaneously.

At a time when so much attention is lavished upon the importance of accountability in marketing, retail curiously is ignored, presumably by those who just can't imagine their brands as anything but a television commercial.

You know, Andy Warhol was not just an artist. He was an artist, as Terry Teachout wrote, who "silk-screened money." (And, by the way, there is a store named after Warhol at his museum in Pittsburgh).

So, the real question is not what we make of retail.

It is, what do *you* make of retail?

What would Andy do?

Successes

In Wal-Mart We Trust. (1/29/03). Exactly how big is Wal-Mart? The answer is spelled out in stunning fashion in a *USA Today* article by Jim Hopkins. It employs "one of every 123 workers and nearly one of every 20 retail employees. Its computer network is nearly as big as the Pentagon's."

It is "the biggest customer" of "Kraft, Gillette and Procter & Gamble." In fact, Wal-Mart today accounts for 17 percent of P&G's total revenues, "up from 10 percent just five years ago." Kraft derives 10 percent of its revenue from Wal-Mart. A total of "450 of its suppliers have opened offices…near Wal-Mart headquarters in tiny Bentonville, Arkansas," and "as many as 800 more such offices are expected in the next five years." All told, Wal-Mart today has "4,300 stores in nine countries and annual revenue near $250 billion."

Indeed, so big is Wal-Mart that it drove "as much as 25 percent of the U.S. productivity gains from 1995–99"—all by itself. It is the single-biggest influence on the U.S. economy since Standard Oil back in the 1800s. So great is that influence that Wal-Mart significantly affects not only U.S. employment and productivity, but product choices and prices.

Wal-Mart influenced P&G to dump Crisco and Jif and focus more on Tide, for example, and doing so "helped P&G boost fiscal second-quarter net income 14 percent year-over-year to $1.5 billion." And while the retailer "says it is committed to well-known brands such as Kellogg's cereals and Tide," it is developing store brands with profit margins "as high as 30 percent vs. 15 percent on brand-name items."

Unstoppable? Right now, Wal-Mart claims "8 percent of all U.S. retail sales, excluding restaurants and auto dealers…up from 6 percent just five years ago." On average, it attracts "100 million customers a week. That's 88.5 million more people than U.S. airlines fly in a week." It "is expected to report nearly $250 billion in annual revenue for the fiscal year ending

Friday—a 15 percent gain from the previous year, despite the so-so holiday shopping period."

However, some predict "Wal-Mart's growth could be pinched as it digs deeper into urban areas where wages are higher, competitors more numerous and scarce land more expensive." Unfortunately, as Wal-Mart slows, so slows America. In any case, observes Prof. Jim Hoopes of Babson College: "If only one company is adding 25 percent of our productivity, it means a lot of other companies are not growing fast enough."

Sears' Happy Returns. (2/7/03). Like every other retailer, Sears is in the business of pushing sales out the door, not pulling them back in. And yet, the retailer has put in place technology that enables it to make money on that which its customers bring back, as reported by Kim S. Nash in *Baseline* magazine (Jan 03). "Returns can actually be profitable," says Prof. Dale Rogers of the University of Nevada at Reno. "It sounds crazy but it's true…It has become an objective for a lot of enlightened firms."

The challenge for Sears, typical of most retailers, is that every supplier has a different set of standards regarding returned merchandise. Some want the stuff "sorted by type of product" and another wants stuff back "only when the pile hits a certain dollar value or number of units." But for Sears, with some 10,000 suppliers and 2,900 stores, the chaos was a real losing proposition, to say the least. So in 1993 it engaged Genco Distribution Systems to put in place "reverse logistics," and "since 1999, Genco has processed at least 23 million returned items every year for Sears."

Genco not only built a database of supplier returns protocol, but also set up three warehouses from which all returns are processed. Sears simply hands the whole arduous process off to Genco. Store personnel just pile up the returns, unsorted, on a pallet and call Genco to come and pick it up. Genco estimates that "centralizing and outsourcing returns can cut in-store labor to about 10 hours per week per store." Annual benefits—increased manufacturer credits, fewer labor hours on the chore, more cost-effective shipping—are pegged at $4 million per year."

Clay Valstad of Sears actually won't confirm exactly the profitability of reverse logistics for the retailer, but confirms: "In addition to recovering significant dollars in vendor credits or through recycling, we are able to recover all the costs of running our reverse logistics program."

Circuit City Success. (4/30/03). Everything changed when Circuit City CEO W. Alan McCollough decided that he wanted his MVT, reports Brendan Coffey in *Forbes* (5/12/03). No, not his MTV. MVT—Multivariable Testing—"a way of testing dozens of variables simultaneously in real-life situations." MVT was first applied by statistician Charles Holland in the early 1960s "to figure out why a certain atomic bomb part had a crippling 85 percent rejection rate." Certainly a fine ambition.

Since that time, Mr. Holland's consulting firm, called QualPro, has applied MVT to help manufacturers find assembly-line problems. Over the last three years, however, his mathematicians are turning their magic to try "to get a handle on the finicky shopper"—and to spectacular effect.

After two, six-week studies in late 2000 and early 2001, Circuit City implemented "changes that contributed to an estimated $300 million in sales for the 12 months ended September 2002." The process started with CEO McCollough collecting some 3,000 ideas from his store-level employees. From those ideas, 15 were selected to be tested in 16 stores, each of which "tried a different combination of the 15 ideas."

The findings were surprising. Having more salespeople to help customers did not help grow revenues. Flat commissions worked better than product-based commissions (the focus turns to what the shopper wants instead of what the salesperson wants to sell).

Ultimately, the retailer dropped commissions altogether, and enjoyed "an immediate 3 percent comparable-store sales rise." Circuit City SVP Jeffrey Wells comments: "What did we learn about ourselves? That our gut stinks." And, observes Mr. Holland: "Vice presidents and janitors are equally likely to have an idea that has a positive impact on a problem." Toys R Us, Staples and Lowe's are also among QualPro's clients, who pay anywhere from "$500,000 to $3 million to run a six-week test of 20 ideas."

Starbucks, But Younger. (5/15/03). With its 222 stores in 11 countries, and $110 million in sales, The Coffee Bean does not expect to surpass Starbucks, as reported by Justin Doebele in *Forbes* (5/26/03). After all, Starbucks has 6,444 stores worldwide and $3.3 billion in sales. However, Victor Sassoon, a former rock promoter who bought the 40-year-old, LA.—based Coffee Bean & Tea Leaf chain five years ago with some partners, is angling to be a worthy "number two" behind Starbucks by plying a different demographic. His target: A younger crowd.

Near the center of that strategy, naturally, is the coffee, which features "a lighter roast" said to be more appealing to younger 'buds, relative to the Starbucks darker coffees. "It's like toast," says Coffee Bean COO Melvin Elias. "The more you burn it, the less you taste the bread." Fighting words, all right. Responds a Starbucks spokesperson: "It takes the great skill and artistry of a master coffee roaster to bring the best coffee in the world to life."

No matter, really, because even more important to The Coffee Bean's success is its "ice-blended coffee concoctions…which can be up to 75 percent milk, powder and non-coffee ingredients." The Coffee Bean actually was the first to sell these youth-oriented confections, and they "account for 45 percent" of its sales.

Armed with this opening, the 45-year-old Sassoon is aiming at launching "280 new outlets over the next few years—targeting the U.S., Spain, Germany and Japan." He needs to raise an estimated $200 million to do that, and an IPO is under consideration. If Sassoon succeeds, The Coffee Bean may not catch Starbucks, but could well eclipse the current "number two" chain, Dotour, boasting $440 million in sales via 1,218 stores, exclusively in Japan.

Monro's Trusty Mechanics. (6/11/03). That's an apparent contradiction in terms that Rob Gross, CEO of Monro Muffler Brake Inc. has turned to his competitive advantage, as reported by James Covert in a *Dow Jones Newswires* dispatch.

In January 1999, when he took the helm at Monro, "which numbers 561 repair shops and 18 dealer locations, across the Eastern U.S.," Gross did something really controversial. He introduced cut-rate oil changes—originally priced at just $13.99, but now at $19.99 are still about two bucks below market. His idea was not to discount to build volume, however. His idea was that the cheap oil change would bring in fresh customers and, with them, new opportunities to build customer loyalty and trust.

"Let's not try to sell them something every time they walk in the door," says Gross, explaining how he persuaded his dealers and mechanics to try the approach. "Don't focus on the size of the invoice—if you do that, you're telling your people to oversell," he told them.

Well, some of his people really didn't like this idea, but they went along with it—and it has paid off. Gross says that customers who came in "for oil changes two or three years ago now appear to be coming in for bigger purchases." Right on strategy. "We're lower priced on oil changes, but we're not lower priced on everything," he says. "Once you build up trust with the customer, price becomes less important in the equation."

Sales increased 21 percent for the fourth quarter, ending March 29, "fueled by double-digit gains across several product and service categories, including a 33 percent increase in scheduled-maintenance services, a 28 percent gain in commercial services and a 26 percent increase in tire sales." Another key part of the Gross strategy, was an investment in his people, "offering some of the best pay and benefits packages in the industry."

The move built loyalty on both sides of the counter: "Our customers like to see the same manager in the store when they come back because they trust them," says Gross. "If they see 'John' behind the counter and they saw him last year, they'll keep coming to see him next year."

Tommy Bahama. (6/24/03). Tony Margolis and Bob Emfield didn't realize what they had realized when they got the idea for a line of tropical "kitschware" in the early 1990s, but they have parlayed it into an enterprise they just sold to Oxford Industries for $325 million, as reported by Ginia Bellafante in *The New York Times*.

"We started kidding around about this guy who didn't have to go home and who never had to leave the beach," explains Mr. Margolis. "When he needed beer money, he'd go into his closet and pull out a shirt, one of many, from a seamstress he'd met in Bora-Bora. He'd sell it to a friend, and make whatever he needed to get by."

That's Tommy Bahama—which (or who?) in the first year ('92-'93) "generated $3.5 million in sales." That tally nearly tripled in the second year and today racks up some $300 million per year across 32 stores. Not bad for a guy who never leaves the beach.

Of course, Mr. Margolis, chairman, spends a good deal of his time in an office overlooking NYC's Bryant Park. And it's precisely that tug—between work and play—that makes Tommy Bahama, Tommy Bahama. "Could he barbecue?" rhetoricizes designer Lucio Dalla Gaperina. "Absolutely. Could he fly around in a private jet? Absolutely."

Could he sell shirts for about "$40 or so more than the average white cotton dress shirt at J. Press"? You betcha. The shirts, actually, only account for about 20 percent of Tommy's take these days. The rest comes "in part from slouchy pleated pants and an emerging line of women's clothes designed by a vanished star of '80s fashion, Christian Francis Roth."

And now that the Tommy Bahama mystique has been sold, some "30 new…stores, selling not just polo shirts and washed silk trousers but plates and bed linens," will "open over the next three years."

CarMax Magic. (8/27/03). The new car business may be choking on its own incentives, but in used cars it's a whole different story—at least for CarMax, reports Earl Eldridge in *USA Today*. Profits at CarMax—which runs 43 big-box, used-car stores in mostly mid-sized markets—reached $95 million as of last February.

The franchise expects to open as many as 44 new stores over the next four years, which should double its sales to about $88 million. Five years ago its stock traded at about five bucks a share, but as of yesterday, the price was $36.99.

Some people laughed when CarMax, www.carmax.com, threw open its doors ten years ago, at the time under the ownership of Circuit City, the consumer electronics chain, which has since spun it off. Well, heck, they had never seen anything like it before so how could it possibly work?

Co-founder and ceo Austin Ligon says he knew it would be a challenge going in, but was confident that persistence would pay off. "It took a lot of time and investment to get the economic model right," he says. He simply believed that consumers would take to the idea of a low-price, no-haggle, quality-guaranteed automotive superstore, where shoppers are invited to search the Internet and in-store kiosks for just the right car at just the right price.

"CarMax," Ligon says, "is the first true retailer of cars. We are not a dealer." Indeed, the standard CarMax store spans 40,000–60,000 square feet, with sister satellite stores (usually 15–20 miles from its standard stores) occupying 14,000 to 19,000 square feet. Inventory ranges from 250 to 500 cars, "none more than six years old."

CarMax has backed away from earlier, larger stores, and is no longer opening new-car stores. Its fortunes have also been helped by AutoNation's withdrawal from the used-car market. Its success, however, has less to do with luck than with insights into consumer behavior.

Automotive economist George Hoffer comments: "They appeal to consumers who don't look for the lowest price but lowest total cost of buying. The cost of buying a car includes the search by going from dealer to dealer, the hassle of negotiating and the fear of being swindled."

Men Who Shop. (12/17/02). "I'll do just about anything to avoid shopping," says John Brown of Cheyenne, Wyoming, as quoted by Kevin Helliker in *The Wall Street Journal.*

But Mr. Brown will drive 100 miles to spend the day at Cabela's, a eight-store, six-state, hunting-and-fishing superstore chain. "I'm like a kid in a candy store here," he says. Women and children—busloads of school-children, in fact—love Cabela's too: "The Cabela's in Michigan is that state's largest tourist attraction, drawing six million people a year—35 percent as many visiting shoppers as all of New York City had in 2000."

In addition to making shoppers out of men, Cabela's seems to prove that, Wal-Mart notwithstanding, "rural shoppers care about more than price. Indeed, they will drive a long way to find ambiance, service and fashion." Selection, too—"six to ten times deeper, especially on high-end goods," versus the typical discount store.

The ambiance is one of museum-quality taxidermy, set "in scenes so authentic that even the droppings are real." Grizzly bears doing battle—stuff like that—occupy up to 45 percent of floorspace. Huge aquariums, too, housed in stores that soar like indoor stadiums.

The service consists of unusually large numbers of clerks, each of whom "had to take 100-question tests on the products they sold." Where fashion is concerned, Cabela's is the only store in its areas that sells high-end apparel, merchandised in upscale fashion. That draws women—as well as men looking for gifts to mollify the wives or girlfriends they may have left at home.

Some actually refer to Cabela's as a kind of Wal-Mart in reverse—not only because of its heavy investment in the shopping experiences versus low prices, but because it tends to bring shoppers to small retailers to obscure locales as opposed to running the mom-and-pops out of business (other than the sporting-goods stores, of course). Cabela's is planning to build more stores, but probably just another 25 or 30.

The upside potential looks huge: "Hunters and anglers spent $70 billion last year and yet there is no national chain of stores devoted just to serving them." Even though the number of U.S hunters declined by 7 percent in 2001, their expenditures increased by 29 percent.

Cabela's does have a competitor in a 25-store chain called Bass Pro, however it tends to operate in urban markets. Currently, each store claims only about $1.25 billion of the total market, but some say the two retailers are looking like the "Coke and Pepsi" of the sporting-goods category. Both retailers go their starts in the catalog business.

Whole Foods' Phenom. (9/9/03). "I believe in free minds and free markets," says John Mackey, CEO and founder of the fast-growing Whole Foods organic-supermarket chain, as reported by Julia Boorstein in *Fortune* magazine (9/15/03). He says his goal is to bring "truth, love and beauty" to his enterprise, as he cites Maslow's hierarchy of needs as the organizing principle of his business strategy. Of those who shop his stores he says: "They want to make a statement about who they are by where they shop."

They are making that statement in ever-increasing numbers. From its humble beginnings in 1978 (the precursor to Whole Foods occupied two floors of a Victorian house in Austin, Texas, and was called Safer Way), Whole Foods, www.wholefoods.com, today has 143 stores in 35 markets. It is not only the largest natural-food chain in America, but also "the fastest-growing company in the fiercely competitive grocery business."

Its same-store sales are up 8 percent over the past two years and its stock has jumped 131 percent over the past three years. Its margins, at 3.1 percent, are almost double those of Safeway, and revenues, at $2.8 billion, "have doubled in five years."

"We're not just about being organic," Mackey explains, noting his stores sell ice cream, candy and potato chips, for example. Indeed, shoppers can buy just about anything they might otherwise find at a mainstream supermarket at Whole Foods—albeit often as a high-margin, premium-priced store brand (which are "the best sellers in 90 percent of their categories)."

High-quality perishables, previously the chain's Achilles' heel, are now its biggest draw, accounting for 65 percent of sales. Key, as well, is a retro approach to purchasing—Whole Foods empowers "regional directors and store managers to choose local products."

Says Mackey: "We're not going to turn down the best product if the vendor won't pay us $10,000." He also says he wants nothing to do with unions, which he terms "highly unethical and self-interested." But above all, he envisions a kind of Starbucksian destiny: "He wants natural foods to become as common as $4 lattes."

Wegmans' Sweet Spot. (11/24/03). "Daniel Wegman lives in fear," opens a *Forbes* magazine article by Matthew Swibel. And why shouldn't he? The article continues: "Thirty-nine of his 65 Wegmans Food Markets are within 20 miles of a Wal-Mart supercenter." Says Danny (as everybody calls him): "There could be trouble ahead…But fear," says Danny, "can be very liberating."

And for Wegmans, it is also very profitable. Wegmans' sales, at $3.3 billion, are up nine percent this year, while operating earnings, at 7.5 percent, compare favorably with "an industry average of five percent." In addition, at a time when 17 percent of all grocery stores closed down last year (often by Wal-Mart), Wegmans is expanding.

Danny Wegman's liberation manifests itself mostly as being just about everything that Wal-Mart is not. His stores are atmospheric (but in a good way). He's got chefs sautéing scrod under hammered-copper stove hoods. Artisan bread is presented as though in a "Parisian open air market." Customer service, as Danny puts it, is "telepathic."

Where Wal-Mart is moving toward self-checkouts, Wegmans keeps its checkout lanes fully staffed. Where Wal-Mart touts low prices, Wegmans stresses both price and quality. That appeals to the Wegmans shopper, who tilts toward "career couples," and who appreciate Wegmans' gourmet items and prepared foods. Indeed, some 40 percent of Wegmans' floorspace takes aim at career couples.

The Wegman's difference is also apparent in the way it stocks its stores. While Wal-Mart is consolidating suppliers, "Wegmans works with 600 farmers to stock its produce section." Here's an interesting one: After deciding that circulars were wasteful, Danny Wegman reverted to "the classic grocer's gambit of underpricing the milk and eggs to get people in the store." He says the move, over time, has caused no loss in sales, while saving "$3 million a year in advertising."

The article notes that Wegmans may be similar to Wal-Mart in its distaste for union workers and the heavy fines it imposes on suppliers who are late with deliveries. But for the most part, Wegmans is winning on differences: "We need to do what Wal-Mart can't," says Danny Wegman. The Wegmans empire, by the way, began in 1916 "with a single produce push-cart in Rochester," New York.

Costco's New Luxury. (11/24/03). Costco is but "20 percent the size of Wal-Mart," but it "has made a monkey of the 800-pound guerilla," reports John Helyar in *Fortune*. Yes, it's true that Sam's Club "has 71 percent more stores than Costco (532 to 312)" but Costco, for the year ended August 31, enjoyed five percent more in sales "($34.4 billion vs. an estimated $32.9 billion)." On average, a Costco store "generates nearly double the revenue of a Sam's Club ($112 million to $63 million)."

Prevailing opinion seems to be that Wal-Mart is unlikely to catch Costco, and here's a key reason why: Costco has cornered the market on what book author Michael Silverstein (*Trading Up*) calls the 'new luxury.' " Costco's target shopper (pun intended) is "a breed of urban sophisticate," who "eagerly spends more for items that make their hearts pound and for which they don't have to pay full price," says Silverstein.

Things like Callaway golf clubs and Starbucks coffee, for example. "Then they 'trade down' to private labels for things like paper towels, detergent and vitamins." Says Costco ceo Jim Sinegal: "Our customers don't drive 15 miles to save on a jar of peanut butter. They come for the treasure hunt."

Wal-Mart, meanwhile, aimed its Sam's Club at its traditional base—the mass middle market, which, by and large would be mystified, if not alienated, by "bargain" T-shirts priced at $39. The Costco customer knows that's a great deal, because the same thing would cost another twenty dollars at a department store. Costco management, meanwhile, knows that "affluent shoppers" today account for 54 percent of warehouse club customers. The bottom line, according to Neilsen, is that the average Costco customer logs 11.4 visits per year, spending $94 each time.

At Sam's, it's 8.5 visits at $78 a throw. Irony is, Sam's management (five ceos over ten years) has tried to catch Seattle-based Costco by copying its "new luxury" positioning. Could it be that no one at Sam's Club has read Sam Walton's book? Hm.

JCPenney-wise Profits. (9/11/03). In a "radical" power shift, retailer J.C. Penney is letting a no-name Hong Kong manufacturer call all of the shots on the house-brand shirts it sells, as reported by Gabriel Kahn in *The Wall Street Journal*.

The result is nearly instantaneous replenishment of the colors and styles consumers are demanding, with no inventory left languishing in warehouses. Basically, J.C. Penney no longer orders its shirts. It is *told* by its supplier—Tal Apparel Ltd.—what it has bought. "That is the future," says Rodney Birkins Jr., vice president of sourcing of J.C. Penney Private Label Brands, Inc.

It is a future that even Wal-Mart's vaunted supply chain system has yet to reach. Although Wal-Mart does open "its computer systems to suppliers," to better track demand and supply, "it stops short of allowing its suppliers to place its own orders." Penney became open to that idea after Tal's Henry Lee, pointed out that the retailer "was holding up to nine months of inventory, twice what most competitors kept." Even worse, Penney often found itself out of stock on "hot-selling items," and burdened with "less-popular models that they had to move at a discount."

Mr. Lee's proposition was that "if he could get sales data straight from the stores, he could take the consumer's pulse and respond instantly." Perhaps even more significantly, Tal, www.tapgroup.com, also test-markets new styles, creating small runs that are offered for sale in, say, 50 of Penney's 1,040 North American stores.

"When you put something on the floor that the customer has already voted on is when we make a lot of money," says Mr. Birkins. In other words, J.C. Penney, www.jcpenney.net, "in effect lets consumers, not marketing managers, pick the styles." Tal's Mr. Lee is now contemplating "a joint venture with Penney that would manage the supply chain for some other manufacturers that supply the retailer." Says Mr. Lee: "I can do all the pieces of the puzzle."

Rubbermaid's Phoenix. (12/30/02). By the time Joe Galli got to Newell Rubbermaid in January 2001, its products had been thrown out of Lowe's and Wal-Mart, reports Matthew Boyle in *Fortune* "This was not a rosy picture," says Galli, who had himself just come off of a dot-com stint, following a "superstar" run at Black & Decker.

But now, by Galli, Rubbermaid is bouncing back, mainly because of an army of young merchandisers who are on the ground and in the stores making darn sure that shoppers leave with some Rubbermaid products—everything from that plastic stuff to Levilor blinds and Calphalon cookware—in their carts.

The "army" is called Phoenix, appropriately enough, and its foot-soldiers are known as Phoenicians. They currently number 573, and are recruited straight out of college, selected based on their aggressiveness and outgoingness more than their academic records. Football captains and sorority presidents, for example.

They go through merchandising boot camp, where they learn the fine art of in-store merchandising, like how "to stack Sharpie pens in just about every department, from electronics to sporting goods." Cross-merchandising! It's not lost on Wal-Mart that those Sharpie pens have 50 percent margins—why not put them in the frozen food department, too?

It's precisely that brand of merchandising energy that has Rubbermaid back in the good graces of Wal-Mart, Home Depot and Lowe's. Galli gets down in the trenches himself, spotting display opportunities that otherwise might have gone to dead space.

His charisma—some describe it as Napoleonic—does, however, rub off on his troops: "One Phoenician designed a three-sided, five-foot-high, wheeled display for tools, accessories and Sharpies, which boosted sales 250 percent. It's now set to be featured in almost 600 Lowe's stores."

The one retailer that doesn't care much for the Phoenicians is Target, which apparently isn't so keen on letting its suppliers create the shopping experience in this particular fashion. Galli, meanwhile, plans to double his Phoenix budget to $100 million in 2003, "hire 600 more reps, and even expand into Europe."

Zingerman's Deli. (10/1/03). What started as frustration for a restaurant dishwasher and its manager has blossomed into a $6.6 million deli with a decidedly different take on creating a food empire, reports David Kiley in *USA Today*.

Ari Weinzweig, the dishwasher, and Paul Saginaw, the manager, opened Zingerman's Deli, www.zingermans.com, in Ann Arbor, Michigan back in 1982, initially out of disgust with their boss' "conventional business model that saw the employees as disposable and food as over-head." Ann Arbor, being a "college town," was a perfect fit for their deli, whose heart is quality food and soul is customer service. However, after its first ten years in business, when success made expansion possible, the part-ners took a left turn.

Rather than open more, or bigger, delis, they opened a "bake-house"—the first of a series of complementary businesses that today includes a creamery, catering, mail-order and, most recently, a full-scale restaurant called Zingerman's Roadhouse.

These businesses are not only integrated (the bake-house supplies all of the other ventures, for example), they add more than $21 million in reve-nues on top of what the deli pulls in. The partners "own a majority stake in the businesses, and carefully chosen partners own the rest." By decade's end, "Zingerman's hopes to have 12 to 15 enterprises, with a chocolatier and coffee roaster vying to be next."

Slow growth, that's right. It's a philosophy rooted in their food, so to speak. Zingerman's even makes its own horseradish, "from roots grown by a local farmer; the grits are whole-grain from a 19th century corn varietal." Their prices are correspondingly "wallet-wilting," for sure.

The deli's service, meanwhile, is not necessarily slow, but it is as warm as it can be, which the partners say is essential (*i.e.*, "Customer service earns the profit because no one *needs* what we sell").

So legendary is Zingerman's service that it has spawned, yes, a training program called ZingTrain, www.zingtrain.com, both for its own employ-ees as well as outsiders. However, for all its success, don't expect to see a Zingerman's Deli in your 'hood anytime soon: "Like I want to be flying to Atlanta to make sure the corned beef is right," says Ari. "If we did that, it means everything we told our employees and partners has been a lie, and there goes the whole idea."

Couche-Tard. (10/19/03). That means "go to bed late" in French, but it also means that American convenience-store retailers will have to start getting up earlier if they want to compete against Alimentation Couche-Tard, Inc., as reported by Bernard Simon in *The New York Times,*

One reason is, the Canadian c-store chain last week agreed to purchase "2,000 outlets owned and operated by the Circle K Corporation," adding to the 2,575 stores Couche-Tard already owns and operates in Canada and the Midwest. You may know these stores as Mac's, Bigfoot or Dairy Mart. But the main thing is, Couche-Tard is re-defining its category by tailoring its stores "to match local tastes" both in terms of format and product assortments.

For example, in Calgary, one C-T store caters to a kids-heavy neighborhood with a store offering "12 flavors of Froster, Couche-Tard's version of 7-Eleven's Slurpee drink." Just a few miles away, in a 'hood with fewer kids and more adults, the store features "about 25 seats where customers can drink coffee and read newspapers." In upscale neighborhoods, the stores stock more imported beer.

In Hispanic locales, C-T provides Latin American brands. To attract women, it was out with "bulky sandwiches" and in with "salads at stores in office areas." That move "increased the proportion of female customers to 45 percent from 33 percent over the last five years."

Recognizing that prepared foods drive traffic, Couche-Tard has partnered with Dunkin' Donuts, Subway and Pizza-Pizza. Understanding that even c-store shoppers like a little pizazz, stores are sometimes dressed up in hunting and space-travel thematics. All of this is a bit radical in the c-store business, where a busy street corner and likely products has been the success formula. That doesn't seem to work so well any more—nor does offering gasoline, because the margins on petrol are not what they used to be.

And, of course, Wal-Mart not only sells gas now but also has "drugstores that stock food and candy" just like a c-store. Oh, but so what? The mastermind of the C-T strategy is one (very confident-sounding) Alain Bouchard, ceo, who says elegantly: "When you know who your customers are, that can give you an edge on the competition."

Blue Nile. (10/17/03). "Everything we do is heresy," says Mark Vadon of Blue Nile dot-com, an online diamonds retailer, as quoted by *USA Today*'s Byron Acohido. "Instead of marketing to women, we market to men. Instead of trying to push our gross margins as high as possible, we sell as cheap as we possibly can. Instead of hiding information, we're all about educating the consumer and making him feel comfortable." That is primarily accomplished via "comprehensive online tutorials" on diamonds.

That is a really smart approach, apparently, as Blue Nile has seen its revenues grow "almost 180 percent to $125 million this year from $45 million in 2000." The growth is particularly remarkable because Blue Nile began life as a $57 million venture-capital backed enterprise in 1999, near the peak of dot-com mania.

But it succeeded by realizing the promise that so many others had only imagined: "Our overhead is low, and we honestly do pass that savings on to our customers," says Vadon. He also says "it would take 150 stores and 1,000 employees" to compete against his business in the offline world.

Instead, Blue Nile has just 115 employees in a 21,000 square-foot office building, located in Seattle. Its inventory consists of "30,000 certified diamonds and 70 settings," with rings ranging "from $700 to $483,000." This idea began for Mark Vadon after his own search for an engagement ring, when "a jeweler…advised him to pick a $12,000 diamond ring on the basis of which one 'spoke' to him."

Right. So, he went online and found a site called InternetDiamonds.com, which used *information* as its sales tactic. Vadon not only bought a diamond, he bought the company, renamed it Blue Nile, and "generated sales of $14 million" in the first six months. Vadon expects he'll to grab an ever-larger chunk of the $5 billion U.S. market for engagement rings. "We don't understand why anybody would buy anywhere but with us," he says.

Hindustan Lever. (10/28/03). Unilever may be struggling overall versus Nestle and Procter and Gamble, but its distribution strategy in India may be saving its bacon, so to speak, reports Cris Prystay in *The Wall Street Journal.*

What Hindustan Lever recognizes is that India's fragmented retail environment provides opportunities not open in American and Britain, for example. The problem in those countries is that retailers have consolidated and are so powerful they effectively "block their suppliers from becoming their competitors." In Britain, "four big retail chains account for 70 percent of Unilever's sales." That pretty much keeps Unilever and every other consumer packaged-goods company in its traditional place.

Not so in India, however, where the retail landscape consists of "small, independent shops that can't complain if Lever starts competing with them through direct sales. And so that's exactly what Hindustan Lever does—franchising some "50 salons in the last three years" through which it sells its Lakme cosmetics brand, www.lakme.com, for example. That business is flourishing, as more Indian women join the workforce.

Plans are to open 200 more such salons over the next three years. They even have a loyalty-card program! Lever's other inroad is door-to-door sales, "taking a page from Avon's book, by bringing its wares directly to consumers. This approach plays very well: "We need expert advice and there's nowhere to get it," says one happy customer. "Shopkeepers can't explain the products well."

Products sold in-home typically "cost about 40 percent more than Lever brands sold in stores," as consumers are willing to pay a premium for the convenience and added-value of expert advice. Hindustan Lever, www.hll.com, hopes to grow this success, having this year added "home, dish and laundry detergents, plus male grooming products and oral care to the door-to-door line."

Right now, its direct sales force numbers 75,000, and plans are "to recruit a million more in the next five years." The company has also "experimented with businesses including a home-laundry service and an online grocery store." Lever does face competition in India from the likes of L'Oreal and Revlon, but for now "Hindustan Lever contributes about 10 percent of Unilever's revenue."

Wal-Mart de Mexico. (9/2/03). Or Walmex, if you will, "is not a carbon copy of its U.S. parent," but it "is the largest retailer in Latin America and...the largest private employer in Mexico," reports Kerry A. Dolan in *Forbes* (9/1/01). Walmex claims "26 percent of Wal-Mart's $40 billion in international sales, the second-largest share after its U.K. operations." And even though "the Mexican retail market contracted 1.8 percent" last year, Walmex profits "grew 12 percent, to $476 million—at 4.7 percent, a fatter margin than the 3.3 percent its parent netted."

"We think Wal-Mart de Mexico is a very good model," says John Menzer, who is president of Wal-Mart's international division, and is already applying Mexican lessons learned to the Japanese market.

The model is to start small, relatively, as Wal-Mart did in 1991 when it initially "formed a joint venture with Mexican retailer Cifra." Wal-Mart actually waited six years before acquiring a majority share (62 percent) in Cifra, and another three years before changing its name. What Wal-Mart acquired from Cifra was a total of "six different formats, including apparel and restaurant chains that cater to the disparate income segments of the Mexican population."

For example, Bodega Aurrera is for low-income Mexicans, while Superarama supermarkets cater to "middle and upper-income customers in urban areas." Then there are the Wal-Mart Supercenters and Sam's Club stores that are pretty much like those in the U.S.

Walmex naturally applies Wal-Mart's vaunted logistics systems to good effect: "Its distribution efficiencies and its leverage with suppliers enabled it to increase its market share among the top four retailers from 44 percent in 1998 to 50 percent in 2002, according to Morgan Stanley."

Walmex, www.walmartmexico.com.mx, also delivers benefits to Wal-Mart's U.S. stores, which now sell flowers and candy from Mexico, not to mention "goods from Mexico for Hispanic customers in the U.S." Meanwhile, "Walmex plans to spend $615 million to open 61 new stores and restaurants" between now and July 2004. Thing is, "there are still 190 Mexican cities with populations of 50,000 or more that don't yet have a Walmex store."

Selling

Shopping Hydrotherapy. (11/21/02). Okay—since you *insist*—we'll write about *Bateau Tar-zhay*—you know, the floating Target store that docked at NYC's Chelsea Piers, at West 23rd Street. Amy Finnerty writes about her shopping experience there in a *Wall Street Journal* essay, and seems to like what she encountered, more or less.

She calls it "an exotic, almost cultish, shopping experience," that begins with greetings from "red-clad, sailor-capped minders," who instantly signal that the shopper is "embarking on something truly hokey." Of Target's crew she writes: "They are a super-vital force of nature, which contributes to my sense that I am being taken to the cleaners as I am escorted to the boat."

She does, however, credit Target with "actually shouldering for the consumer some of the cognitive and emotional burden of gift selection," in that "the merchandise has been pre-edited, down to 92 items…that are presumably Target's idea of what Manhattanites will find irresistible and affordable this year…Instead of racks of accessories, for example, we are presented with a powder-blue shearling hat, scarf and glove set-priced separately from $9.99 to $12.99—as a *fait accompli*."

Target proper actually carries some 50,000 to 60,000 SKUs. Other items include a "turkey fryer, a distressed leather blazer…a desktop refrigerator…some dowdy luggage and holiday-themed housewares."

The presentation is similarly Spartan: "They have placed prototypes of their mysterious selections in transparent cases, some of them embedded in synthetic, iceberg-like structures," she explains. "Customers can't touch or smell the microfleece pjs or men's suede jacket, but are instructed to take one of the written descriptions provided for each and present it at Merchandise Pickup.

Manhattan shoppers, Target seems to have concluded, will be more open-minded than most people about virtual shopping and unorthodox delivery systems."

Target also figured out that a captive audience, combined with a limited opportunity, adds up to a pretty effective sales incentive. The retail space itself is only about "the size of a large, two-bedroom apartment," only 150 people are allowed in at a time, just 92 items are available and the boat leaves on December 1st. As a shopper, Finnerty concedes, she was "lulled by the gentle listing of the vessel and the subliminal exhortation to 'Buy Now.'"

In Clubland. (1/21/03). If you think you are saving money by using a supermarket club card, think again, suggests Katy McLaughlin in *The Wall Street Journal*. McLaughlin's five-city, loyalty-card test revealed that stores without club cards were less expensive—sometimes big time.

In Chicago, the same basket cost five percent less at card-free Treasure Island, than at Safeway's Dominick's, where you only have to give up your name, address, e-mail and phone to get a "Fresh Values Savings" card. In Dallas, Albertson's "Preferred Savings Card" rang up eight percent higher than SuperTarget, with no such card.

The most impressive gap occurred in Atlanta, however. The same items purchased with a Kroger "Plus" card cost 29 percent less at—you guessed it—Wal-Mart, with no card in hand. Okay, you say: That's Wal-Mart. Right. But competing against Wal-Mart is often the rationale used by competitors for starting a loyalty-card program in the first place. Not that they like to admit this, preferring instead to suggest that their stores do not compete on price alone. For example, Safeway says its card-holders also earn frequent-flier miles and Albertson's says its card program makes donations to local schools.

Reality is, apparently, that the cards only make shoppers *feel* like they are getting a deal, when in fact the prices on everything else are jiggered to favor the retailers. The margins are further padded by the 10 percent of shoppers who refuse to trade personal information for discounts, with the difference going directly into the retailers' pockets.

Shoppers are catching on, however, as some are logging on to a grass-roots Web site called nocards.org. E.K. Valentin, a professor at Weber State University in Utah, meanwhile, says a poll of nearly 1,000 card-users in his state shows most consider the loyalty programs to be a gimmick. Valentin is set to publish a report on his findings in the Journal of Applied Research in the spring.

Considered Set. (1/30/03). How do you shop? Professor Barbara E. Kahn has you all figured out, as described by Virginia Postrel in *The New York Times.* "The composition of the set of final possibilities can have subtle effects on choices," she wrote in *Grocery Revolution,* with coauthor Leigh McAlister. That means "brand choices can be influenced without changing the content of the consideration set."

The heck? The "consideration set," also known as the "evoked set" is "the brands in a product category that the consumer remembers at the time of decision making," as defined by K. Douglas Hoffman in his book, *Marketing Best Practices.* In other words, when you think of yogurt, two or three brands spring immediately to mind—say, Dannon, Stonyfield and Yoplait (depending on where you live, of course). You basically don't even see—or consider—the other brands on the shelf, and once you've made your brand choice, your flavor selection is the picture of brand loyalty.

So, it's really important for a brand to be in the considered set, although it is possible to change the set and with it, the consumer's choice. For instance, as Kahn and McAlister point out, if the yogurt were organized by flavor and not brand, shoppers would choose flavors first and brands second. This theory actually has played out in Australia, where "grocers arrange meats by the way they might be cooked...The result is that Australians buy a greater variety of meats.

Word Salad. (2/25/03). Words are helping some restaurants increase profits and compete more effectively against the casual-dining chains, reports Joyce Cohen in *USA Today.* Words like "chewy" and "velvety" and "lacquered" and "infused" work especially well, says one expert. When words like those pop up on menus, people tend to order whatever it is they are meant to describe, and that can be very good for an eatery's bottom line.

In some cases, that's because the description sounds more "expensive." Choice words also help persuade diners to order higher-margin items. According to menu consultant Banger Smith, a little strategic menu word play "can boost a restaurant's profit as much as 15 percent."

In this world, a steak becomes "a rib-eye of fire," featuring "a zesty rub of blended spices and herbs." Sales go up when a generic "lobster tail" is called "Caribbean Lobster Tail." When a Midwestern restaurant chain reinvented its "chicken sandwich" as a "half-pound chicken burger," it succeeded in "steering beef eaters toward the more profitable chicken offering."

A restaurant consultant meanwhile advises that slugging "appetizers" as "things to share" makes the cash register ring where otherwise it might not. "Some people don't eat appetizers because they're afraid they won't be hungry for the entree, but it is always fun to share something," says Jim Laube of www.RestaurantOwner.com.

Here's a good one: An Oakdale, NY caterer upscaled pigs-in-a-blanket by re-naming them Wieners Wellington. Sometimes, however, it's not just the words, but a subtle ingredient shift that makes the difference. A Staten Island caterer turned chicken potpie into pheasant potpie, for example. His "chicken tartlets" meanwhile were transformed into "spicy Thai chicken tartlets in crispy lotus cups with fire-roasted peanuts." He reports that a "40-cent addition to a dish—complemented by a new name—can increase the price by $2."

Discount Luxuries. (2/6/03). Hammered by tight wallets and pinched by chains, upscale restaurants are turning to "stealth discounts" to keep themselves in the black, reports Katy McLaughlin in *The Wall Street Journal*. The restaurateurs don't call them discounts, though. Of course not. Not coupons, either (even worse).

No, the white-linen set is cutting prices with "gift certificates," to be slipped in, discreetly, with the bill. Or, "club cards," not unlike the shopper loyalty cards offered by supermarkets. Still others are signing on with www.iDine.com, where the trick is a credit card that simply includes a refund on the diner's statement.

Such deals—which regularly whack about 30 percent off a bill—are to be had at some of America's finest restaurants—"Olives in Boston, MK in Chicago and 21 Club in New York," to name just a few. The Internet, naturally enough, is pretty much at the center of this universe. Really determined diners have found ways to combine as many as three online offers for a really hefty price cut. A site called DinnerBroker.com offers up to 30 percent off by booking online, while Restaurant.com sells "gift certificates" at half price." Then there's always eBay.com, where Restaurant.com certificates are auctioned at still lower prices.

Some diners have elevated the opportunity into a "parlor game" of sorts, a contest to combine as many offers as possible. Wait staff, for the most part, plays along, poker-faced. "Our policy is to be very discreet," says Bill Blum, general manager of Saddles, in Sonoma, California, where the staff undergoes special training so they don't bat an eye.

Of this new reality, Michel Jean, owner of Provence in NYC comments: "You want me to stay alive, or you want me to go into bankruptcy?" Actually, he's reacting to news that a diner had used not one but two discounts at a single meal, taking 40 percent off. However, he admits: "Who doesn't need help selling their early tables these days?"

Sandwich Savant. (7/22/03). Consumers "have made the connection between upscale coffee and upscale sandwiches, which makes them spend more for sandwiches," says consultant Michael Whiteman, as quoted by *USA Today*'s Jerry Shriver. The food industry, in turn, has made the connection that their customers want "more affordable and comforting dishes." Says Whiteman: "The guy who used to spend $30 to $35 for lunch with wine isn't there anymore, So it's better to have a creative sandwich and iced tea and have that person in your restaurant."

And so, "the energy and resources that chefs used to pour into $25 entrees now is directed toward $12 sandwiches." Actually, this idea is neither recession-driven nor anything new for some sandwich chefs, such as Nancy Silverton of Campanile, www.campanilerestaurant.com, in Los

Angeles, where she has been drawing "capacity crowds for seven years to the Sandwich Night she stages every week." Her creations start at $14 and feature "rustic sourdough slices, topped with braised artichoke, soft ricotta, pine nuts and currants. Or sweet Gorgonzola, roasted radicchio, spiced walnuts and honey."

Ms. Silverton is at the high-end of a trend that also consumes Arby's, the quick-serve chain, which recently added a "gourmet-style Market Fresh Bistro." Whiteman observes: "People are seeking out new flavor profiles…The bland no longer leads the bland." Good line, eh?

Even the descendants of the Earl of Sandwich, who is said to have invented the delectable in the 18th Century, are getting into the act, having announced "a chain of sandwich cafes," www.earlofsandwich.co.uk, that will "feature about a dozen $5 sandwiches," the first of which will "open around Thanksgiving at Walt Disney Resort near Orlando."

Unchain America! (9/24/03). That's the slogan of a national association of independent restaurants that is trying to help local eateries compete against the chains, as reported by Catherine C. Robbins in *The New York Times*. The association, known as the Council of Independent Restaurants of America (CIRA), www.ciraonline.org, coordinates a range of "promotions, charity events and cooperative advertising" via a program called The Originals.

The Originals, so far, have chapters in 12 regions. In Arizona, for example, it's The Tuscon Originals, www.tucsonoriginals.com, where one of its members, Don Luria, periodically invites middle-school kids to enjoy a free meal at his upscale Cafe Terra Cotta, www.cafeterracotta.com. He calls the program "Kids Dine Out" and says that most of his guests have never eaten anywhere but in fast-food or chain restaurants. The kids get to try "unfamiliar foods like calamari and duck," and "are encouraged to ask questions about the menu and learn basic restaurant etiquette." He says that "the kids' eyes totally open up."

The Albuquerque chapter, www.albuquerqueoriginals.com, this weekend "will provide the food at an annual equestrian charity event, allowing the chefs to show off their cuisine to the young professionals who attend."

Says Philip Cooke, executive director of CIRA: "We work to the best of
our ability to assure the survival of independent restaurants in America."
In addition to Albuquerque and Tuscon, The Originals have chapters in
Birmingham; Chicago; Columbus; Indianapolis; Kansas City, Mo.; Flint,
Mi.; Madison/Milwaukee, Wis.; St. Louis, Minneapolis and Washington,
D.C.

Case-Ready Meat. (2/17/03). Chops and steaks are joining the drum-
sticks, as the realm of case-ready meat expands from chicken to include
meat in America's supermarkets, as reported by Constance Hayes in *The
New York Times*. Case-ready means that the meat is cut, trimmed and
labeled before it gets to the store. It is packaged, usually, in deep trays with
a tight, plastic film across the top and a kind of gas—typically a combination of oxygen and carbon dioxide—keeping the flesh flush. Wal-Mart,
which turned to case-ready meat exclusively in September 2001, also uses
a saline treatment to "keep the bloom on the meat."

Ah, Wal-Mart. Again. Some say it is Wal-Mart's case-ready conversion
that is driving the supermarket trade to follow suit. It is, after all, less
expensive and more efficient to get rid of meat cutters who earn about a
thousand dollars a week as well as eliminate extraneous product handling
and moving. "It flows really, really well," says a Wal-Mart spokesperson of
the case-ready regimen.

However, some retailers say it is not Wal-Mart but customer demand
that is driving the case-ready trend. "Wal-Mart is doing it for other reasons," says Mark Greenberg, president of Wakefern Food, which buys its
case-ready supply from Philadelphia-based Pennexx Foods, a $60 million
concern that is half owned by Smithfield Foods.

"Our position," says Greenberg, "is we are looking to determine what
the customer is looking for." Noting butchers cannot keep the same 24/7
hours maintained by some supermarkets he explains: "We want to make
sure that when the customer comes in, the full variety is there." Comments
Michael Queen, CEO of Pennexx: "Business is really, really growing."
Indeed, he predicts his company's sales will triple by next year.

Yvette's Test. (6/4/03). Determined to find an edge versus the many third party, discount travel websites, a San Francisco-based boutique-hotel operator is putting some personality into its pitch, as reported by Sheila Muto in *The Wall Street Journal.* That personality has a name—*Yvette*, to be exact—"an animated character who will help travelers find hotels among the company's 24 properties in the San Francisco Bay Area that best fit their personalities and needs. She will then link consumers with like-minded local residents, who offer up things to see and do."

Chip Conley, CEO of Joie De Vivre Hospitality, Inc., says he expects Yvette will help promote his properties on a basis other than price. "There are other important determining factors about what is the right hotel for you," he says, noting that Joie De Vivre will continue to match the lowest prices offered by the discount sites. Yvette, meanwhile, will play "matchmaker" via a series of five questions, such as "What kind of people do you most admire?" The choices are: "work hard/play hard; sensible/practical; welcoming/friendly; established/affluent; dynamic/vibrant; subtle/refined; visionary/artistic. If you'd like to take Yvette's test: www.jdvhospitality.com/test

The overall plan is to shift some of the sales volume from the third-party sites to the Joie De Vivre site. Currently, the company derives about 10 percent of its bookings from the discounters, and 4 percent from its own site.

The goal, according to Mr. Conely, is to increase the number of home-grown reservations to 10 percent by 2005, which would boost the bottom-line because the bookings would be free of the 25 percent commission charged by third-parties. A Cornell University professor rains on Yvette's parade, however: "There's always going to be a group that's always price driven," he says. Of course, not one of them went to Cornell.

Skinner's Winners. (6/17/03). Having perhaps gambled and lost a few too many players to smaller, nimbler casinos, Harrah's is revamping its vaunted *Total Rewards* program with bigger, better prizes, reports Christina Binkley in *The Wall Street Journal.*

Harrah's, as you may recall, made a big splash with its "frequent gamblers" program, when it launched in 2000, primarily because its program involved data mining of its customer files. This enabled Harrah's to better target and entice its most profitable players.

Today, the program has 27 million members. Trouble is, the casino's rivals quickly copied key elements of the Harrah's offering. Even a small, regional, outfit called Ameristar Casino managed to siphon off small-time gamblers who play slots regularly—say, four times a week—but only spend about $20 at a time.

Harrah's mistake was requiring its customers to cash in their rewards immediately—but these players "couldn't earn enough credits fast enough to buy any goodies." So, under Harrah's new program, they can "save up credits to buy cheaper items, such as $5 coupons at restaurants and complimentary valet parking."

Harrah's is also extending its rewards from "slot-machines only" to include "blackjack and other table games." It also offers bonus points for placing off-peak bets. Says Harrah's CEO Gary Loveman: "With this bonus-credit apparatus, we can really adjust the juice. The loyalty points are a function of customer profitability."

The real play for Harrah's, of course, is for the high rollers, and the operative attraction is the prize structure. Under the original plan, "bonus points" could be cashed in for various casino amenities only. The new plan, as pictured in a 35-page catalog, includes more intriguing fare, such as naming a horserace at Louisiana Downs or riding in a pace car at the Winston Cup. Earning the former would require making about $600,000 in bets, and the latter, $9 million.

Harrah's is also targeting women, with incentives such as a Macy's shopping spree, an evening with Chippendale dancers, and a visit to Elvis' Graceland. However, for all its sophistication, A University of Nevada economics professor sees *Total Rewards* as pretty primal. "Players like to receive positive reinforcement—pats on the back, in effect," observing that Harrah's concepts "go back to B.F. Skinner www.bfskinner.org and all the pigeon studies."

The Buyosphere. (12/19/02). That's the term used by book author Thomas Hine to describe the expanding universe of places at which "to hemorrhage money," as reported by Pia Catton Nordlinger in *The Wall Street Journal*. Nordlinger reviews Hine's book, called "*I Want That!*," in which the author says the buyosphere has been growing for centuries, and has had a profound effect on humanity. Shopping, he says is a "defining characteristic" and an "expression of our complex relationship to things."

For example, "Hine observes an elderly woman making an arduous, but, as it turns out, routine trip to her local Wal-Mart." Ostensibly, she's buying "personal items and gifts." In fact, says Hine, she's demonstrating her independence and importance to her family. Sure, she could do that in other ways, but, remember, she is living and breathing in our buyopshere.

Incidentally, Hine raises—and rejects—popular notions that women's brains are somehow "hard-wired" for shopping or that shopping is a modern-day expression of female "gathering" relative to male "hunting." He instead points out that women write most of the family checks, and marketers feed right into—and perpetuate—that reality.

However, Hine also takes a shot at Wal-Mart, which would have to be at the very center of the buyosphere: "That such a store could provoke apathy instead of amazement is a perverse tribute to the plenitude of our consumer society and the weakness of the emotional ties that bind us to the many objects in our lives. Never before has so much seemed so dull."

Indeed, Hine writes: "The challenge for the sellers, is to make each piece of this material plenty mean something, so that shoppers will want to make it part of their lives."

Future Store. (6/19/03). As soon as you walk through its doors, you pick up a small computer, swipe your shopper card through it, and up pops a shopping list of the items you typically buy, as well as the day's specials, reports Annick Moes in *The Wall Street Journal*. This "keyboard-size computer" is equipped with a touch screen and a barcode scanner, enabling you to ring up your purchases as you shop—no checkout lanes, here.

Meanwhile, the store's central computer is tracking which products you pick up or put back, as well as the items you buy together, and in what order you buy them. This not only ensures that the shelves remain fully stocked, but also "trigger commercials on one of the store's ubiquitous video screens related to products that are selling."

It all sounds very futuristic, but it is also very real. This store of the future, www.future-store.org, is located in Rheinberg, Germany, and is an experiment by Metro AG, "the third-largest retailer in Europe and the fifth-largest world-wide." It is attracting shoppers from cities as far away as Frankfurt and Mainz (about two hours by car), as well as the interest of rival grocers like J Sainsbury, and Rewe Zentral AG.

That this experiment is happening in Germany is no coincidence, either, as the country is "one of the world's most difficult retail markets," where "retail sales have stagnated for 10 years." That's owing to a collection of factors: "In Germany, laws limiting shopping hours, discounts and competition, plus a general social unease with consumption, discourage people from buying even in good times."

That's why "private consumption" accounts for only 59 percent of Germany's GNP, relative to 70 percent in the United States, for example. Metro is betting that a better shopping experience is just the thing to pull Germany out of its economic torpor. As Metro spokesperson Albrecht Truchess puts it: "The question is: Do you capitulate as a retailer or do you develop new concepts?" However, the other question is whether technology is the answer: "Three years ago, German grocery chain Rewe built a similar test store and found customers liked interacting with people more than computers."

One thing's for sure—Metro's high-tech merchandising is complex, involving some 39 co-sponsoring companies. It is also far from perfect, at least for now. Its ultimate success depends on RFID microchip tags to track in-store traffic, which at 50 cents apiece, remain way too expensive to apply to all but a few items in the store.

Pricing Power. (9/15/03). Was a time, not so very long ago, when Michael Eisner was deemed "a managerial genius" just for jacking up ticket prices at the Magic Kingdom's gates, observes Geoffrey Colvin in a *Fortune* essay. Ah, the power of pricing. It turned Disney around, back in 1984. Today, however, Disney's price premium ($52) versus rival Universal Studios ($51.95) totals exactly five cents. Disney's not alone here, Colvin continues: "Consider that Coke costs no more than Pepsi—and neither costs any more than it did 20 years ago."

The sluggish economy is often fingered by the frustrated as the reason prices can't be raised. Colvin says that's part of it, but so is a "worldwide abundance of capital," that has resulted in a "global overcapacity" that sits "on top of prices like an anvil." He goes on to give a host of other reasons why pricing power has gone poof—all of which are rooted in the same place: The Internet.

Yes, the Web has made it easy for new competitors to upend established players. The eBays and the Monsters have cold-cocked newspapers, draining off their "greatest profit source—classified advertising." The papers didn't even see them coming.

On the ugly underside, Colvin writes, the Internet "lets guerilla warriors" demonize brands as never before—McDonald's, Nike and Coke, most notably. The Web, as we all know, makes it easy to steal—and distribute—pirated intellectual property, be it a melody or a medicine, at a fraction of the original price.

Online information meanwhile puts consumers on a direct path to the lowest possible prices, whether they buy online or not. But what drives price, online, is not always price. Monster and eBay, Colvin notes, "have plenty of pricing power" because they are just so darn popular and people keep coming back—a phenomenon Colvin calls "increasing returns." Oh, and there is one more "price-crushing influence" that is not a dot-com, *per se*, and that, writes Colvin, is the most important company in America, Wal-Mart."

Prices & Loyalty. (12/19/02). "A one percent price increase at Amazon reduces sales there by about .5 percent," reports Hal R. Varian in *The New York Times*, "but a one percent price increase at Barnes & Noble means a 4 percent sales decline—eight times as large."

Wow. The difference, Varian suggests, is that Amazon has invested in building customer loyalty. "Of course," he continues, "all that investment in customer loyalty is expensive, and loyalty doesn't necessarily translate directly into profit." It does, however, lay bare the two basic types of online shoppers—those who will pay a price for reliability and service, and those who just want the lowest possible price.

The two types are also in evidence in the offline world, of course. The difference is, their behavior is much more pronounced and easier to observe online, both because of transaction data and transaction costs: "Searching for the lowest price used to be a costly activity; now it can be performed automatically by shopbots," Varian notes. "Changing prices used to be costly for merchants, but now it can be done with a keystroke."

Observing such unvarnished shopping behavior is at the center of research by economists Michael R. Baye, Patrick Scholten and John Morgan featured on a Web site, appropriately named: www.Nash-Equilibrium.com.

Retailer behavior is also on display. For example, a statistic called "relative dispersion" captures the difference between advertised and average prices, which is 11 percent online—meaning that "about 32 percent of the advertised prices for a given item vary by more than 11 percent from the average price." The explanation is that online retailers—even more than offline retailers—bait-and-switch their customers with artificially low prices. The economists also track "Internet competitiveness," which is "an aggregate statistic of various indicators of how competitive online prices are."

Currently, according to the Census Bureau, "online purchases in the United States totaled more than $11 billion in the third quarter this year, up 34 percent" versus a year ago. Total retail sales for the period were $827 billion.

Retail as Banking. (2/14/03). Washington Mutual likes to call itself WaMu, which sounds more than a little like Wal-Mart. No coincidence there, most probably, as reported by Linda Tischler in *Fast Company* (Mar. '03).

Just listen to WaMu CEO Kerry Killinger: "In every retailing industry there are category killers who figure out how to have a very low cost structure and pass those advantages on to consumers, day in and day out," he says, adding: "Within a year, we'll be put into a different category, as a high-growth retailer of consumer financial services. We'll even start losing the banking label. Then you can put our numbers up against all of the retailers in the country, and you'll have one of the top-growth stories."

Killinger seems well on his way to making good on that prediction, on the strength of a highly-focused product offering and a very different kind of retail banking experience. WaMu's strategic focus is on the middle class—the same base on which The Home Depot, Target and Wal-Mart were built. It's a market that is "underserved and overcharged," observes Jay Terjera, a Ragen MacKenzie bank analyst. The "one-two punch" for WaMu is home loans and free checking—the two "most important products for Main Street America," Terjera notes. On these two products, WaMu relationships are built.

The retail environment is equally essential to WaMu's customer construction. A WaMu "store" bears little resemblance to a traditional bank—no teller windows or velvet ropes. Free-range, khaki-clad sales associates handle no cash—dollars are dispensed by cash machines only. WaMu associates instead chat up customers and cross-sell products.

That, WaMu believes, is the key to customer loyalty: "After one year, 96.4 percent of customers with four products are still with the bank, while only 75.5 percent of those using one product are still around." Of course, some folks still prefer a closed door to WaMu's open season. The bank's acquisition spree and rapid growth are also causing various kinds of growing pains. However, with its 7 million customers, WaMu appears to have the markings of a very big brand indeed, maybe even the Wal-Mart of banking (…but isn't Wal-Mart the Wal-Mart of banking? ☺).

Cheap Trick Fashions. (10/10/03). Taking a page from the "scarcity strategy" handbook written by high-fashion brands, mid-market apparel-makers are building desire by making consumers wait for the latest styles, as reported by Eileen Daspin in *The Wall Street Journal*.

Where once it was only the most exclusive and expensive fashion houses—like, say, Hermes—that had the juice to put their customers on waiting lists for scarce commodities, the likes of Banana Republic are now creating "fashion moments" by denying their customers what they want.

"When we sell out, we sell out," teases Deborah Lloyd, Banana Republic's evp for product design and development. "It adds to the allure."

So far, the gambit is working for a certain $198 Banana Republic blazer, shipments of which were limited to just 5,000, "no more than half the normal run for such a product." And, of course, the jacket was promoted heavily to make sure that demand would outstrip supply!

Meanwhile, a "trendy jeans maker" called Paper, Denim and Cloth, www.blaec.com, "just launched a 300-per-style special collection…made from hand-picked cotton." As a trend, this one is not limited entirely to fashion, however. Ford created a waiting list for a new Mazda model while the "New York Jets briefly tried charging fans $50 just to keep their place on waiting lists for season tickets." Guess it didn't work for them.

Whatever the category, the wait-list mavens crow that they don't even need advertising if they can place the product with enough influential editors, shops and A-list celebrities." For example, a Santa Barbara boutique simply put a blown-up photo of "Cameron Diaz wearing a new $168 Hello Kitty necklace" before it was available and—*voila*—created a waiting list of 20 customers.

Not every retailer is so enthusiastic about such tactics, though. Some complain that "wait lists are creating image and hype at the expense of sales." As for their customers: "What's the point?" says one who was informed of a waiting list for a handbag at Saks. "It blew my mind. How about, 'Let's make more and bring down the price so everyone can have one?'"

Sample Sales. (11/25/03). It used to be that "only the most chicly acquisitive were invited," but today even men are showing up at so-called "sample sales," at which designers unload that which they could not otherwise sell, reports Ginia Bellafante in *The New York Times*.

This open season on bargain designer clothes actually is in high season right now, a fact that is known to a great many shoppers thanks largely to websites such as www.nysale.com and www.dailycandy.com

The events "typically take place in downtown or garment district showrooms." As these places do not have changing rooms, "it is common to see women grabbing at cocktail dresses in their underwear or trying to squeeze chiffon halters over their turtlenecks." This makes for an atmosphere of "emotional abandon in which many injudicious purchases take place." It also created a fun photo op for the *Times*, which carried a great picture of a woman in a frilly dress with her jeans down around her ankles.

The shopping experience is perhaps best described as "primal," leading psychologist Ellen Haimoff to advise shoppers "to identify the primitive feeling of the hunt" to help avoid making purchases they later regret. She notes that shoppers don't enjoy the luxury of "leaving the situation, sleeping on it and coming back the next day."

One of the most common traps is buying something only because someone else seems to want it more than you do. And one of the most interesting developments is that some designers are now feeding directly into sample-sale mania. Designer Alice Roi, www.aliceroi.com, for example, "had miniskirts made just for her sample sale because they were popular this season and she had not included any in her collection."

Women Who Hunt. (12/17/02). "At the beauty counter," reads the headline of a *New York Times* article by Cathy Horyn, "it's bait, hook and reel them in." Maybe that means it's the women who are hunted, but try telling *that* to the women whose trophy was a $25 gift card at Bergdorf Goodman in New York City.

Wait—discounts on cosmetics at Bergdorf Goodman? Yes, but Bergdorf suggests that the gift card promotion isn't really a discount, but, well, a kind of service to its shoppers. Uh-huh.

Whatever it is, it appears to be working. "Twenty-five dollars makes the difference," confirms one shopper. Bergdorf actually had to lock its revolving doors because women were getting stuck in them in their mad rush to get to their gift cards. Bergdorf CEO Ronald Frasch says the gift cards have turned its basement-level beauty area into "our best performing area of the store." Sales are up 50 percent versus a year ago.

"The biggest challenge," he says, "was to take a high impulse-purchase business and make it a destination business." The gift cards also enable

Bergdorf to add names to its database, "for a relatively small investment." Ah-ha.

The gift cards actually are not the only draw at Bergdorfs, where shoppers are also served cranberry vodkas and canapes. "It's really entertainment that has to ring the register now," says Ed Burstell of rival retailer Bendel's, where women are treated to free facials, manicures, eyebrow shapings and even "a free lip analysis to see what kind of personality they have…"

Over at Macy's, shoppers were recently offered "12-inch televisions for $15 with a $50 cosmetics purchase." All in all, says Allan Motus, editor of cosmetics newsletter *The Informationist*: "This has been the most highly promotional season I've seen in the business." The beauty business, by the way, totals $37 billion.

Fetch-it-Yourself. (11/19/03). Only about "five percent of all online sales last year were picked up in-store," but that percentage is expected to increase, according to Forrester Research, www.forrester.com, as reported by Chao Xiong in *The Wall Street Journal.*

One reason is, shoppers want to avoid paying shipping costs. Another is, they can get the item faster. And, of course, they can return it on the spot if the merchandise doesn't meet expectations. But the greatest driver of this online-offline trend appears to be the retailers themselves, who enjoy opportunities to register impulse sales every time one of their online customers sets foot inside their stores.

Indeed, REI, the sporting-goods retailer, "estimates that a third of online shoppers who pick up their items in stores spend an additional $90 before they walk out the door." The retailer has been taking that dynamic to the bank since June, when it introduced a fetch-it-yourself policy. Today, REI says "almost a third" of its online sales are picked up in-store. They're not alone: Circuit City says "about half of its online shoppers now opt for in-store pickup."

Such shopper response has retailers hoping that fetch-it-yourself policies will provide some fresh momentum to online shopping, sales which total more than $36.9 billion this year, according to comScore Networks.

That's 18 percent more than last year, but less than the 30 percent gain posted in 2002.

Thing is, relatively few retailers are prepared to make the idea work, in some cases because customer service reps are based in Bangalore, for example. However, Sears is so confident of its online-offline offering that it guarantees items will be waiting for shoppers when they arrive at the store. And Circuit City boasts that online orders are ready for in-store pickup within 15 minutes, 99 percent of the time.

Filene's Doghouse. (7/14/03). Two sisters from Newton, Massachusetts have been banned from all 21 Filene's Basement stores because they returned too many items and lodged too many customer-service complaints," according to an *Associated Press* dispatch. Nancy Singer says she and her sister "received a letter from the chain's corporate parent in May, telling them they were no longer welcome in the stores."

Normally, observes Kathleen Seiders, a Boston College associate professor of marketing, retailers avoid taking such measures because of "bad publicity and bad feelings."

Naturally, the sisters immediately took their complaints to the press, making public the corporation's letter, which read, in part: "Given your history of excessive returns and your chronic unhappiness with our services, we have decided that this is the best way to avoid any future problems with you and your sister."

Comments Ms. Singer: "The sales staff is always telling you to go ahead and buy it, and return it if it doesn't fit or look right." She speculates that the ban is related to complaints she made to Value City Department Stores, Filene's corporate parent, in April, "about comments from a Boston store manager."

Value City CFO James O'Grady denies that any particular incident led to the Singer-sisters ban, saying only that customer bans are "extremely rare," but that the sisters had brought back an "incredible" number of things. He complained that the women consumed too much of sales-associate time with their returns and complaints.

Professor Seiders sees the ban as a function of retailing's tough times, and seems to hint that it may be a sign of things to come. "Balancing low profit margins and customer service levels is problematic, to say the least," she says, and notes that retailers increasingly are tracking customer spending with an eye on identifying which customers are not as profitable.

Customer Rage Management. (9/17/03). "There are certain kinds of problems that are never going to be solved through technology," says Scott Broetzmann of Customer Care Measurement and Consulting, as quoted by Jane Spencer in *The Wall Street Journal.*

He's talking about satisfying angry customers, and how so many companies only make matters worse by attempting to automate a solution. "You can't ventilate to a machine," he says. Problem is, even if the issue is resolved, the customer usually is left feeling angry anyway. Reason is, most customers simply want an apology, and that, of course, requires a human touch.

To be precise, 59 percent of customers want an apology, but just 5 percent say they have ever received one after registering a complaint. That's according to a new study by Customer Care Alliance (Virginia) that also found 45 percent of households experienced "at least 'one serious problem' in the past year, with a product or service, and more than two-thirds of those customers had experienced 'rage' over the way the incident was handled." Such frustration levels appear to be on an uptick, as a 1976 report had logged "serious problem" respondents at just 32 percent.

What has changed, according to the study's authors, is that three decades ago most complaints were made by mail, where today most customers simply pick up the phone. More often than not, the most irate customers "wind up getting bounced between agents because the first-line contacts aren't empowered to resolve more serious complaints."

So typically, the more serious the complaint, the more numerous the bounces—and the more numerous the bounces, the less likely is the customer to be satisfied. What a mess. And, to top it all off, there's this: "Ninety percent of the angry customers reported they shared the story with a friend."

Concepts

Not JetBlue. (11/6/03). Sure, they offer low-fares and high-style, but Delta's Song Airlines, www.flysong.com, is finding its own flashy way to let potential passengers know that it is just as hip as the next airline, reports Motoko Rich in *The New York Times*. Starting tomorrow, and for the next six weeks, the fledgling airplane outfit will run a store in SoHo, at 98 Prince Street—on the very same block as the Apple Computer and Prada stores.

Like its neighbors, Song hopes "to use retail space to sell an image." Says Song spokesperson Stacy Geagan: "We want people to say 'An airline is doing that?' I thought it was a clothing store...or a gallery.'" Or a night-club: The store will celebrate its opening tonight with a party that has Moby, Grace Jones, Drew Barrymore and Fabrizio Moretti on the A-list.

Michael Rock of design firm 2x4, which had a hand in designing the Prada store, tries to explain it: "You don't really change the function of the thing itself," he says, "but you change the perception of the function of the thing and you differentiate the surface of it." Spoken like a true artist. Anyway, Song's store will showcase "sleek electronics and installation art."

For example, a work by Howard Goldkrand features "streaming video of skies running continuously past a panel that looks like the side of a plane." Also on display are "airline seats, X-Box game systems...and air-plane windows stocked with retail items from Kate Spade," who designed Song's flight attendant uniforms.

You can even buy Song's airline food there. In SoHo. Comments Alex Calderwood of design firm Neverstop, which designed the Song store: "That communicates a sense of confidence and spirit." Indeed, Julie Lasky of *I.D. Magazine* says the whole idea is to evoke emotions, and not neces-sarily sell products: "It's taking people out of the notion of an airplane and linking them to a sense of adventure, comfort and things that have become general experience."

What do the folks at JetBlue think of all of this? Not much. Unlike Apple, says JetBlue spokesperson Gareth Edmonson-Jones, Song is neither known nor loved, and therefore is not likely to attract many shoppers. "I think it's just putting the cart before the horse," he says.

Saks for Tots. (2/25/03). The thing about department stores is that they used to have departments, suggests a *Wall Street Journal* article by Amy Merrick and Joseph Pereira. Like, toy departments. That started to change when category killers—like toy retailers—began picking off department store shoppers with bigger selections and lower prices. Department stores such as Saks Fifth Avenue caved into the likes of Toys R Us and, yes, Wal-Mart. They closed their toy departments—and with them lost a reason for shoppers to shop their stores.

Apparently, department stores cannot live on apparel and home furnishings alone. Saks says it is planning to lease anywhere from 600 to 3,000 square feet of space inside most of its 245 stores to FAO Inc., operator of the FAO Schwarz, The Right Start and Zany Brainy toy-store franchise, itself a Chapter-11 notch on the belt of the category killers.

Saks CEO George Jones says this makes sense because toys appeal to the retailer's core customers—mothers with children. "We hope that moms, when they get in their cars with their kids will now be more likely to go to our stores versus our competitors," he says. Unlike the big-box retailers, the Saks selection will be strictly upscale and higher-quality—things like "exclusive Barbie merchandise and high-end Steiff stuffed animals typically not found at discount stores."

Some observers wax the Saks potential by recalling the era before the 1970s, when "department stores were a chief destination for shoppers," even holding "product demonstrations...and elaborate play areas." Says Thomas Conley of the Toy Institute of America: "I can remember companies in those days complaining about the power Sears and Macy's were wielding in the toy business." Of course, no one really expects Saks to pose a serious threat to Wal-Mart, which sold some "$15 billion in toys and sporting goods in fiscal 2001," while "FAO's sales were a paltry $162.5 million in the same year." But hopefully, Saks—and FAO—might start do a little better in the profits department.

China's C-Stores. (11/3/03). So fierce is competition among Shanghai's convenience-stores that 7-Eleven won't risk getting bloodied, at least for now, reports Leslie Chang in *The Wall Street Journal.*

Just last year, there were but 1,500 c-stores in Shanghai, but today there are 3,500. Walk down some city streets and you'll find as many as "two or three convenience stores on a single block."

Such growth is driving China's $500 billion retail sector, "but it is also driving down gross profit margins, which have declined "from 21 percent several years ago to 15 percent last year" (compared to a global baseline of 30 percent).

Such realities have the likes of 7-Eleven cooling its jets. "Let them fight it out in Shanghai," says Bob Jenkins, 7-Eleven's vice president of international, "we'll go in after the war is over." That would appear to suit Wang Jinlong, president of the 486-store Liangyou chain, just fine. Mr. Wang cut his retailing teeth leading Starbucks' "expansion into 20 countries, including China," and is now in charge of Liangyou's c-stores under the brand name, "Buddies."

Mr. Wang's plan features store designs that set Buddies apart—floor-to-ceiling shelves (creating an impression of abundance) and 5-foot-wide aisles ("to inspire leisurely strolling and impulse-buying"). He is also "installing computer systems to allow store managers to check inventory and analyze sales data." Perhaps most important, Mr. Wang is empowering his store managers to decide what will work best in their own stores.

"In the past there was a lot of pressure to be orderly," says Hu Fusheng, a store manager. "We could not develop our own strengths." His sales are up, and, chainwide, Buddies is tracking a same-store sales increase of 25 percent in the first nine months of this year. Plans call for opening "50 new stores and 100 renovated ones" by year's end.

Underground Restaurants. (3/12/03). Down that street, up those stairs, behind that door…in apartments, basements and even back-yards…illegal eateries run by "homeless" chefs "abound across the United States," reports Janelle Brown in *The New York Times*. "They are filling a niche that isn't filled by restaurants," says Jim Leff of www.chowhound. com. Underground restaurants, he says, operate "in areas where there are no restaurants, doing it at lower price points, or serving traditional dishes that restaurants are afraid to serve because they are too unusual."

Sometimes the underground restaurants are born of economic neces-sity—chefs who have lost their jobs or who simply can't manage the start-up costs of a legal place. For others, like Lynette (she reveals her first-name only), who runs *Mamasan's Bistro* out of her San Francisco apartment, it's also a matter of self-satisfaction: "I've worked in restaurants for years, and dealing with the public is a beast," she says. "You don't get to edit who comes into your space, and it becomes a very sterile exchange of goods."

Adds Michael Hebbe, who runs *Ripe* in his Portland, Oregon living room: "The kitchen is demeaning. You cook for people you don't see. All you hear from guests is 'this is undercooked' or 'this needs to be redone.' That environment doesn't seem sustainable or healthy, which is why the staff turnover at restaurants is so incredible."

While Mr. Hebbe says his restaurant is "profitable," it is, yes, also ille-gal, operating as it does outside the realm of health and safety inspections, or liquor licenses. Says Jack Breslin of San Francisco's health department: "If no one is looking over my shoulder to see how I'm storing, processing and serving my food, the greater the risk of something bad happening."

Sometimes the joints get busted, but more often it is the guests who need the cuffs. Lynette says her CD collection has been pilfered and Mr. Hebbe complains that his white carpets get trashed. Such has given Lynette momentary thoughts of turning legit; reveries stopped cold by the $250,000 she estimates it would cost to do so. "I do it for love mostly," she explains, adding, "I don't want to boast that I have an illegal establishment in my house, but this is how artists survive."

Nascar's Hotel. (11/4/03). That would be Best Western, which just inked a "$10 million, three-year sponsorship deal…to become the 'official hotel' of Nascar," reports *USA Today*'s Chris Woodyard. The deal involves a "Nascar-themed guest-loyalty program," as well as "special room rates…a sweepstakes" and promotion of the alliance "in advertising and on the Web site."

Well, why not? Some "10 million" fans attend Nascar races each year "at any of the 118 Nascar-sanctioned tracks in 38 states." Best Western has 2,202 hotels in the U.S. alone.

But the big idea is not just to sell more hotel rooms to the many die-hard Nascar fans who follow the circuit from town-to-town. The heartbeat here is the idea that a little Nascar loyalty-dust will rub off on Best Western, and that the hotel chain will get more business overall as a result.

Says Best Western International ceo Thomas Higgins: "Many Best Western guests are already Nascar fans, and our association with the sport will help create opportunities to attract new customers."

Echoes Brett Yormark, Nascar's vp of corporate marketing: "Other hotels have dabbled in the sport before, but the only one that has been fully integrated is Best Western. For them, it's not as much about travel during the race weekend. It's the ability to tap into our 75 million brand-loyal fans."

Beginning next year, Best Western will even add a logo to the Michael Waltrip team's No. 15 Napa Chevrolet. Says Nascar fan Gordon Carlson of the Best Western-Nascar link: "We love it. I stay at Best Western all the time." The "we" refers to the three other fans with whom he is Best-Western bunking. They've decorated their quarters with an inflatable racecar and "life-size cutouts of Dale Earnhardt Jr. and Matt Kenseth."

Harry's Shoes Ltd. (6/27/03). Sixty-six male movie stars have worn pairs of Harry's Shoes to the Oscars over the past two years—even though the footwear is not yet for sale, reports Cecilie Rohwedder in *The Wall Street Journal*.

It's all part of a buzz-before-business strategy being played out by one "Matthew Mellon, the 39-year-old scion of one of America's wealthiest families, and husband of the co-owner of Jimmy Choo Ltd., the "ultra-trendy women's shoe" brand. That's the extent of his fashion pedigree—his family is much better known as bankers, petroleum moguls and benefactors of institutions of higher learning.

But what Mr. Mellon may lack in fashion and design experience he more than makes up in celebrity connections, and he is hoping to take those friendships straight to the bank. Basically, he is putting prototypes of his high-end creations on the feet of the likes of John Travolta, Denzel Washington and Elton John.

He's been working on this style of product placement for couple of years now—giving the shoes to his celebrity billboards for free, of course. His idea is to build some buzz before his fashions go on sale in earnest, which won't happen until later this year. His hope is that when men see male stars wearing these shoes they will buy them too. In other words, he's imagining a Michael Jordan effect, but with very expensive dress shoes.

Some observers have their doubts. "Men," says Anthony Noguera, editor-in-chief of Arena, a U.K. men's fashion magazine, "are less influenced by what other men are wearing. They are not going to go to the store with a cutting from a magazine." However, if the celebrity angle doesn't snag them, Mr. Mellon is expecting that the comfort factor will. Men "increasingly crave comfort in footwear," studies show, and Harry's shoes (named for Mr. Mellon's grandfather, Harry Stokes) "look conservative enough to be worn with a suit, but have rubber soles, making them as comfortable as sneakers."

A total of 2,000 pairs of the shoes have now been manufactured and will go on sale this fall "at only a handful of stores that include Los Angeles boutique Fred Segal, London department store Harvey Nichols and Saks Fifth Avenue's branch in Saudi Arabia." Prices range from U.S. $370 to $500.

The Warhol. (8/6/03). "The people who have the best fame, wrote Andy Warhol, "are those who have their name on stores. The people with very big stores named after them are the ones I'm really jealous of. Like Marshall Field." Warhol, who died in 1987 but who would have turned

75 today, wrote that in his book, *The Philosophy of Andy Warhol*, as cited by Terry Teachout in a *Wall Street Journal* essay.

Warhol actually got his wish, sort of, via The Andy Warhol Museum, www.warhol.org, in Pittsburgh, "whose online store hawks Warhol soap, calendars, wrapping paper, silk scarves, night lights, salad plates, change-of-address cards and boxer shorts." Called *The Warhol*, it is open every day from 12:00 p.m. to 12:15 p.m. ☺

Teachout suggests that the mistake many people make about Warhol (other than misquoting him on that fifteen-minute thing) is thinking he was an artist. Writes Teachout: "He was, instead, a preternaturally shrewd operator who transformed Marcel Duchamp's anti-art into glossy gewgaws suitable for mail-order merchandising. He silk-screened money." In the process, he created a "universal language intelligible to all men in all conditions."

Henry Ford's Vision. (11/21/03). In his lifetime, Henry Ford was mocked for his lack of formal education, but today he is praised for his 74-year-old museum of 650,000 artifacts that teaches history by making it real for its 1.5 million annual visitors, reports Jeffrey Zaslow in *The Wall Street Journal*.

Among the displays are the 1961 Lincoln Continental in which John F. Kennedy was killed, the blood-stained wooden rocking chair in which Abraham Lincoln was shot, and a test-tube containing Thomas Edison's dying breath...about which one visitor says: "It makes me realize that he was a living person who breathed."

That's exactly what Henry Ford wanted visitors to realize. He began his collection after being publicly humiliated for his lack of historical knowledge during a 1919 libel trial against the *Chicago Tribune*, which had called him an "ignorant" anarchist. When asked by the defense for the date of the Revolutionary War, Ford incorrectly guessed 1812.

Nice try, though. "He was made out to be an imbecile," says Ford Bryan, a former Ford Motor Company employee who knew the man. And so, convinced that history books were "mostly bunk," but believing that the "history you can see is of great value," Henry Ford began what many people at the time thought was an eccentric collection, but that is now generally praised by museum curators as "visionary."

J.F.K.'s car actually was leased by the U.S. government from Ford, and was returned to the company. Lincoln's chair was purchased at auction by Mr. Ford for $2,400 in 1929. Thomas Edison's last breath was captured and given to Ford by Edison's son. Also at the museum is the bike shop where the Wright Brothers built their airplane, the house in which Noah Webster wrote his dictionary and—get this—"a letter from bank robber Clyde Barrow praising Ford's products as getaway cars."

The museum's president, Steve Hemp, calls the artifacts "compressed evocations" and continues to collect objects that represent moments when America "fundamentally changed," such as the Rosa Parks bus. Set on 212 acres, The Henry Ford, www.hfmgv.org, as the museum is known, recently underwent a $60 million renovation, and enjoyed a 35 percent increase in attendance last summer.

El Deejay. (9/4/03). That's *el dj*, to be precise, and it stands for Extra Large Digital Jukebox—and it is just that, as reported by Johanna Jainchill in *The New York Times.* It is basically a souped-up personal computer that enables users to choose from 26,000 songs, in mp3, as converted from 1,798 compact discs.

It is a major draw at an East Village, New York, bar called Hi Fi, where patrons gladly feed dollar bills into it in exchange for three songs on a weeknight and two on a weekend. "People want to impress their friends by picking the most obscure thing they possibly can," says Galven Polivka, a bartender. Certain songs actually are flagged as "overplayed" to avoid embarrassment (don't even think of choosing *Yellow* by Coldpay, for example).

This newfangled jukebox was the brainchild of Hi Fi's owner, Mike Stuto, who stocked it with cd's from his own collection. He says simplicity is the difference between his technology and other mp3 jukeboxes, "which typically come pre-programmed with a choice of 200 popular cd's and allow additional songs to be downloaded from the Internet by customers."

With his jukebox, customers simply use a trackball and keypad to peruse their options randomly or alphabetically. He carefully notes that all songs were copied from purchased recordings, not downloaded via the web, and that royalties are paid on all played songs.

So popular is his jukebox (the hangtime to hear your song is said to be up to three hours) that Mike is now planning to market "a software program to equip home computers with similar capabilities, and a commercial version of the jukebox for bars." The home version will cost about $20 and be available online within the next month or so at www.eldj.com. The commercial version has not yet been priced, and will be produced on a customized basis. "I'm addicted, totally addicted," says one enthusiast, adding, "This has finally caught up with what people are doing on a normal day."

Joint Tasting Rooms. (10/12/03). Napa Valley is "the epicenter" of "collective tasting rooms"—the "latest attempt by wineries to grab new customers", as reported by Randall Benton in the *Sacramento Bee*.

The concept actually is driven by smaller wineries that, for one reason or another, can't manage to host tasting rooms independently. One reason is it's just too darn expensive. Another is, some of them are so small they don't even have wineries, let alone tasting rooms (their wines are contract-manufactured). Sometimes zoning laws and remote locations get in the way of having a tasting room, as well.

All of those problems are solved, however, by co-op tasting rooms such as Vintner's Collective, Napa Wine Merchants and Napa Wine Company, where customers can sample any number of wines from different makers. At Vintner's Collective, www.vintnerscollective.com, which "has 38 different wines on hand," the price is "$10 for four wines," or $15 if you want a logo glass with that. Napa Wine Merchants handles 12 producers, and the charge is $5 for any three wines.

Napa Wine Company, www.napawineco.com, meanwhile, is a little different because it also makes wine for some 85 clients—22 of which are "available in the adjoining Cellar Door, the company's tasting room." A daily menu "offers four tiers of three wines each, ranging from $5 to $20 per group." Some of the brands are well-known, such as Jones Family Vineyard, Fife Vineyards, Joel Gott and Pahlmeyer.

Randy Mason of Mason Cellars says the setup is perfect for his enterprise: "I can't afford a winery. It's a way to get the Mason name out and to get the wine tasted." Of course wine buffs, the collective concept avoids Napa Valley traffic crawl as well as "hopping in and out of the car to get from one winery to another." Also in this game is Wineries of Napa Valley, featuring eight wineries.

Cupcakes! (11/5/03). "It's not about any particular decade—the 50s, the 70s," says Jennifer Appel of the Buttercup Bake Shop, as quoted by Julia Moskin in *The New York Times*. "It's about a return to childhood, whenever you grew up."

Jennifer actually first discovered cupcake-power back in 1996, when she and her then-partner Allysa Torrey casually made a batch using leftover cake batter, and decorated them with buttercream magnolias. Today, the Magnolia Bakery, on NYC's Bleeker Street, sells 3,000 cupcakes a day, yielding $40,000 a week. Even "at midnight, the line still snakes out the door and tourists pose for pictures, proudly holding cupcakes frosted in pale green and lavender for the cameras."

After midnight, that's right—and it's not an aberration: "The kids come in after school, but they aren't the reason we stay open until 11 p.m.," says Mia Kozicharow of Crumbs, where mostly grownups indulge in "more than 20 variations, including Boston cream, jelly doughnut and cappuccino."

Meanwhile, over at the Little Pie Company, they have cocktail cupcakes—that would be the "mojito cupcake, with lime and rum flavorings inside and green lime and mint frostings." Just don't eat and drive.

Fran Sippel of Brooklyn's Downtown Atlantic bakery says cupcakes are indeed an emotionally charged concept for many adults. As Julia Moskin puts it: "They start remembering how their mothers sent them to school on their birthdays with cupcakes packed in a cardboard shirt box." That about nails it. A bakery called Kitchenette goes right for that jugular with its version of "the packaged Hostess cupcake, right down to the squiggle of white icing on the top…"

Out-of-towners are sometimes less impressed, though: "I know you could never sell these in Michigan," a college student says to his visiting parents. "People would just look at them and say, 'I could make those at home!'" Sure, just buy the Buttercup Bakeshop cookbook.

Lollipop Lab. (4/9/03). Dylan's Candy Bar in NYC is not only the world's most expensive candy store and a celebrity magnet, it is a showroom for new sweets for Mars, Topps—and, yes, Wal-Mart, as reported by Donna Fenn in *Inc.* (Apr '03). Mars "chose Dylan's to launch a line of 16 new flavors of Skittles, and the Topps Company is planning to roll our a newfangled lollipop there."

Just one month after Dylan's featured Hershey's Kisses in "new colors of foil" (and displayed in an eight-foot tall Kiss that cost $12,000 to create), Wal-Mart made shelf space for the line extension. Comments Ira Friedman, vice president of new product development at Topps: "They make a statement for candy unlike any other retailer."

It's a statement made by one Jeff Rubin, who launched Dylan's Candy Bar dylanscandybar.com in mid-2001, in partnership with Dylan Lauren, the daughter of Ralph. Some folks laughed when the 9,700-square-foot first opened its doors. "Most people told me 'you'll never make enough to pay for it," Rubin recalls. The cackles stopped as the sweet of tooth formed lines "that stretched a city block." Rubin today claims an average sale of $14.50, compared to about "$4.25 at mall-based bulk candy stores." He crows: "This is the most expensive candy store in the world."

Its customers include Spike Lee (Jolly Ranchers); Jerry Seinfeld (Bit-O-Honey); and Cindy Crawford (Goetze's Caramels). However, just as important as its celebrities and its sales is Dylan's idea to give "Mars, Hershey, Dubble Bubble and Pez each a 'store within a store' that enables them to display a broad range of products." As a result, notes Rubin: "When buyers from Wal-Mart and Target come to town, they come here and they find everything." Look for Dylan's Candy Bar to open new stores in New York, Texas and Florida later this year.

Jake's Ice Creams. (12/2/03). This ain't no Cold Stone, no Ben and Jerry's...this is Jake's Ice Creams and Sorbets, www.jakesicecream.com, a fledgling franchise of four stores in the Atlanta area, that 40-year-old Jake Rothschild expects to grow to 25 stores over the next five years, reports Ann Carrns in *The Wall Street Journal*.

Jake opened his first store about three years ago, with a $350,000 investment and a point-of-difference centered largely on "a homey atmosphere with couches, fireplaces and bookshelves." Indeed, it's the atmosphere that seems to be the main draw for Jake's franchisees, whom he recruits by word-of-mouth.

"I love that Jake's wants each restaurant to take on the look and feel of the neighborhood," says Kyle Jenkins, who adds: "It requires more from a franchisee, but customers will be more loyal to you." Jennifer Johnson, who was Jake's very first franchisee agrees: "The excitement for me is having a place that's community-based and feels unique."

Jake's franchisees build on that feeling by hosting fundraisers for local charities as well as book group meetings, "both of which benefit the community while helping to spread the word about Jake's." The question for Jake is whether that grass-roots, warm-and-fuzzy feeling is enough to compete against much larger competitors, such as Cold Stone Creamery, and Ben and Jerry's.

His answer, actually, is no, it's not. Jake's business model stirs "fast casual" soups and sandwiches into the mix, which he says results in an average ticket of $9, "significantly higher than ice cream-only shops."

Jake's upfront fee to franchisees totals $50,000 and "stores pay five percent of sales in royalties." That compares to $30,000 and royalties of 1.5 percent for a Ben and Jerry's, for example. His franchisees are only too happy to pay the premium for "the chance to grow with Jake's and help mold the business."

Says franchisee Andrew Burke, whose home-grown recipe for carrot-cake ice cream may be adopted chain wide: "In a couple of years, all this will be set in stone. You won't be able to have that kind of impact." Jake, meanwhile, estimates that his franchisees have the potential for sales of between $40,000 and $65,000 a month, and…can recoup their investment in as little as 18 months."

Gadget Shack. (10/30/03). RadioShack Corp. is hoping to re-energize its 7,100 U.S. stores by being first-to-market with innovative electronics, targeted to consumers on a by-store basis, reports Gary McWilliams in *The Wall Street Journal.*

Part one of the strategy is spotting trends sooner and working more closely "with inventors of small, innovative gadgets to jointly develop products." Says RadioShack ceo Leonard H. Roberts: "There are a lot of entrepreneurs who have patents but no manufacturing capacity…We want to match entrepreneurs with money, with manufacturing. That's how we want to be a force in the marketplace."

To that end, RadioShack "recently hosted 250 electronics developers, from tiny start-ups to industrial giants such as Philips Electronics NV, at its Fort Worth, Texas, headquarters." The retailer also "says it will free up space at a RadioShack factory in China for new ideas, and invest its own money in innovative products." Andy Berman, RadioShack's vp of new-business development comments: "We're metamorphosing the company to become more of a leader than a follower."

Part two of the RadioShack strategy calls for plumbing "the demographic profiles of its stores" and customizing its distribution accordingly. So, if a store is located in a college town, for example, it might go heavy on mp3 players.

"RadioShack has invested an awful lot of money in trying to understand who the shopper is down to the individual store," observes Tom Costello, svp of retail sales at Philips Consumer Electronics N.A. However, the question, for some, is whether RadioShack, which at the moment is heavily dependent "on the mature wireless-phone market," can deliver the goods.

"The strategy is attractive," says Robert K. Lifton of Medis Technologies Ltd, www.medisel.com. "They have to demonstrate to themselves and the world that they can carry out and implement it."

Murder Burgers. (11/11/03). At the First-Way Deli, Coochie Cervantes uses about 250 pounds of beef to make about 500 burgers a week, as reported by Alan Feuer in *The New York Times*.

People come from all over, he says, to enjoy one of his burgers, made of a "half a pound of ground beef mixed with bread crumbs, Worcestershire sauce, adobo spice mix, milk, eggs and a dash of Accent season cooked to succulence atop the skillet and served on a kaiser roll with onions, relish and secret sauce."

The First-Way Deli sells these burgers—known as The Murder Burger—for just $4.25, and that includes fries and a 20-ounce drink.

Yes, the Murder Burger. That name, as you might imagine, is even more legendary than the sandwich itself. Some say the name is rooted in the violent past of the Bronx neighborhood where the First-Way Deli is located. Indeed, "there were 40 homicides reported in the local precinct," although that was ten years ago. This year, there have been just six killings, so far.

Thing is, the Murder Burger dates back some 20 years, leading some to suggest its name is connected to a shooting that happened right outside the deli's doors back in the 1980s. But then there's the most tantalizing mythology. There are those who say that the man who invented the Murder Burger was himself a murderer (and they're not just the folks from PETA).

Okay, so you want the real story? The Murder Burger was invented by Thomas Colon Sr., who actually no longer owns the First-Way Deli. He son, Thomas Jr., says his dad "got the name from his customers," who said that the burger was so filling that "it was like their stomachs had been murdered." As one patron puts it: "You eat one, and the burger kills your hunger." Get it?

Sadly, the Colon family never made a killing on The Murder Burger. These days, Thomas Jr. is a gypsy cab driver. But who wouldn't kill for a brand legend like that one?

Allah's Pizza. (11/10/03). Even though it is the multi-billion reconstruction contracts awarded to the likes of Halliburton and Bechtel that make the headlines, it is more than likely the entrepreneurs like Walid Mahmoud who will make or break Iraq's economic future, suggests a *Wall Street Journal* article by Yochi J. Dreazen.

Walid is making that future by making pizzas, an art he learned while visiting Italy in the late '80s, and perfected over a wood-burning oven at a pizza parlor owned by his cousins in Amman Jordan.

In fact, Walid was setting a table at the Amman eatery when he heard that Baghdad, his hometown, had fallen. Having long dreamed of opening his own pizza parlor, he scraped together some "dough" and in June of '03 "opened a small pizza shop under an Italian flag decorated with Arabic writing."

He picked his spot with care, in a so-called green-zone, populated by "thousands of American occupation officials." He decorated the place with the same kind of "high wooden tables" typical of Italy's pizza shops, and hung up a framed photo of the Statue of Liberty.

Things went so well that an American official gave him a cell phone so he could take phone orders. By September, he was raking in $1,000 in profits a week—a huge sum by Iraqi standards. But then terrorist bombings at the nearby U.N. compound and Jordanian embassy put Walid's shop back in the danger zone, and these days he's barely getting by, and worries about what will be if the Americans leave the city altogether.

He says he hopes to hang on by building "ties with U.S. companies," but acknowledges the uncertainties ahead: "Even pizza is in Allah's hands," he says, in Arabic, but with an Italian accent.

Hybrids

Grocerants. (1/3/03). No, not consumer packaged-goods executives complaining about slotting allowances again, but "grocery restaurants," an emerging hybrid of upscale dining experiences situated in ordinary supermarkets, as reported by Pooja Bhatia in *The Wall Street Journal*.

These are really fancy restaurants, with white tablecloths, pricey wine lists and celebrity chefs. They tend to reside within smaller, independent groceries, and are intended both to boost profits and differentiate images. They capitalize on U.S. consumer trends toward less cooking and more dining out, as they take old-fashion ideas like the drugstore soda fountain into a whole new dimension.

So far, the trend is really only a boomlet. Just "12 percent of grocery-store renovations included installing a restaurant of some sort" in 2001, although that's "up from 4 percent in 1997." However, some suggest the eateries are a key reason that "grocery store profit margins are up nearly 60 percent over the past 10 years, to 2.2 percent," as recorded by the Food Marketing Institute.

The restaurant game is most definitely working for Marty's Fine Foods and Wines, a Dallas-based store, which has grown at 20 percent annual rate since it opened a bistro in 1996. "We knew it would be synergistic with our business," says Larry Shapiro, the owner.

Other happy groceranteurs include Minnesota Grille, at a Byerly's in Roseville, Minnesota, where grocery items are promoted via the menu! They put pot roast and wild rice soup on the menu in hopes people might buy them in the store if not order them at their tables, for example. A Wegman's in Rochester, NY, put its restaurant, called Tastings, upstairs, and "has an exposed-brick interior, state-of-the-art open kitchen and the imprint of a famous chef."

It apparently also has a great view of the parking lot. An Ohio super-market meanwhile sprouted a "tea room" complete with "porcelain tea service and dainty sandwiches." Skeptics say the whole idea of fine dining at your local grocery store is batty, especially in today's economy. True-believers have something else to say about it: "The supermarket," comments consultant Howard Solganik "used to be America's pantry; now it's America's kitchen."

Bricks and Flips. (2/13/03). In a $100,000 media deal, the pages of *Surface* (the magazine) will be rendered in the rooms of Surface (The Hotel), as reported by Motoko Rich in *The Wall Street Journal.* This is something else again. Under the deal, the hotel's lobby and top-floor suites will serve as "revolving showrooms for new furniture and room fixtures," as "fashioned by top-name designers." The rest of the rooms will also be "filled with limited-edition fixtures and furniture prototypes," but "in a more-permanent collection." Everything will be for sale.

The magazine's editors, says Riley Johndonnell, editorial director of *Surface*, will "evolve beyond editing two-dimensional pages to curating three-dimensional spaces." The $32 million hotel is currently under construction, and will offer 117 rooms on 20 floors. Set to open in September, it is all-glass and "surrounded by tenement buildings" in Manhattan's Lower East Side. The *Surface*-Surface connection actually was made by Will Candis, "a publicist and former manager of Hotel 17, a one-time welfare hotel in New York that marketed itself as a down-and-out experience for young-artists types." Candis introduced the hotel people to the magazine people.

And, yes, the *Surface*-Surface partnership is "also looking to set marketing deals with high-end name brands that can sprinkle their products throughout the hotel...Mr. Johndonnel says the magazine wants to work with major advertisers," such as Prada, Gucci, Panasonic and Studio Minotti, the Italian furniture-maker. He cautions, however, against going overboard: "It's not a positive experience if you feel like you're being marketed to at every moment," he says. In addition to the $100,000 it will pay to *Surface* (the magazine), Surface (The Hotel) is giving the magazine "a small equity stake" and will "also pay annual licensing fees."

Lucky Magazine. (11/18/03). It publishes "almost no articles...no advice about relationships" and "no celebrity profiles," but it is "the hottest magazine in the land," writes David Brooks in a *New York Times* op-ed essay. It is called *Lucky,* and it calls itself *The Magazine About Shopping.*

Making good on that promise, Lucky is laden with "pages and pages filled with pictures of shoes, lipstick, perfume and handbags." And writes Mr. Brooks: "It's so peppy and chipper it makes going down the Hallmark card aisle in the drugstore feel like a trudge through Germanic philosophy."

Or, perhaps, a sit-down with one of those traditional, exclusive and elite fashion magazines, which Brooks classifies as the "nonsmiling" kind. You know what he means...the models with the "blank or haughty" or "catatonically bored" expressions...the despondent staring into space. All "because, you know, happiness is so middle class."

However, in Luckyland, for its 900,000 readers, there is instead "an aggressively democratic" sensibility, devoid of any "fashion hierarchy...authority figures," or "social elite. There's just the happiness of the local mall...Anything can be cool," Brooks writes, "if you want it to be...Moreover," he continues, "the distinction between upscale and downscale is exploded. *Lucky* exhibits $500 pants side by side with stuff you could find at Wal-Mart." He adds: "*Lucky* appeals to the modern sort of shopper whose consumption patterns don't conform to her income level."

Mr. Brooks sums up the republic of *Lucky* like so: "Nobody is above me and nobody is below me. We are all equal and we are all *Lucky.*"

She House. (3/17/03). Sears Roebuck and Women's Entertainment, a cable network, are partnering to produce a TV show in which viewers first vote on the decor of a million-dollar home and then have a chance to win the abode in a sweepstakes, reports Amy Merrick in *The Wall Street Journal.* Comments Lee Heffernan, marketing chief of Women's Entertainment: "Every network is giving away a house lately, but we are the only network engaging the viewer in an interaction to decide the design."

The show's format calls for decor choices to be interspersed during a movie, with viewers voting online for their favorites. AOL Time Warner's TBS has done something similar, called *Dinner and a Movie*, in which on-screen recipes are featured during a movie.

For Sears, *She House* is a chance to showcase its Kenmore appliances, while building its appeal to women in a way that its sponsorship of Bob Vila's remodeling show, *Home Again*, could not. That show was about "heavy-duty carpentry" and was more of a showcase for Sears' Craftsman tools.

The new show, which will air Friday nights, July 11 to September 26, is more about decorating tips and meant to give a lift to the Sears appliance line, which lately has been losing ground "to the home-improvement warehouses. While Sears is still the industry leader, its market share in appliances has slipped to 39 percent from a high of 41 percent in 2001." The retailer hopes to boost both its top-of-the line appliances as well as some of its more budget-oriented products.

Sears' rival, Lowe's, meanwhile, has been sponsoring a home decor program on TLC for the last three years, *Trading Spaces*, in which neighbors redecorate each other's homes. Sounds kinky. A spin-off, called *While You Were Out*, has meanwhile was snapped up by Home Depot last year. TLC makes its way into 85 million homes, relative to Women's Entertainment's 51 million.

But Women's Entertainment is pouring somewhere between $2 million and $3 million into its new show, and Sears is said to be "contributing nearly $1 million, including merchandise donations and advertising." Sears VP of brand management, Andy Ginger, is sounding sanguine about the new Sears strategy: "When you shop for an appliance it's like shopping for a new car—you haven't done it in a while," he explains. "The attraction is learning about the new features."

Boutique Boozers. (4/30/03). Hip Manhattan retailers are hoping that in-store bars will entice shoppers to spend like, well, drunken sailors, suggests a *USA Today* article by Donna Freydkin. "Stores now recognize that if they can get you to tromp through and to maybe stop by and drink a margarita, you'll stay longer," explains Paco Underhill, an expert on shopper behavior. "We are more time-poor than money-poor, so having a nice place to eat and drink extends the visit, just like adding a food court to a shopping mall stretches out time (and money) people spend in a mall," he says.

Like a mall food court these in-store bars are not. At Nicole's (10 E 60th Street), where designs by Nicole Farhi are sold, part of the draw is "a long, luminescent bar where you can get close to your invariably stylish neighbors." Says one patron: "This is just a refined drinking experience...It's like Origins meets a Zen spa—the music, the openness, the whole ambiance makes it really relaxing. And I love her clothes."

Hipper yet is Decollage (23 Eighth Ave.), described by one of its owners, Heather Rich, as being like a "social club." She says: "It sort of brings you back to Paris in the 30s. We want you to feel like you're in someone's home and we want it to be very intimate, but everyone eventually ends up having a drink in the kitchen."

Or a smoke, perhaps. At Alfred Dunhill (711 Fifth), in addition to offering "four kinds of top scotch," shoppers can retreat to a "walk-in humidor and member's only smoking lounge." Anyone can buy a cigar there, but if you want to light up you need to pay up—an annual membership is $1,000 or a minimum of $5,000 in purchases.

Lunettes et Chocolat (25 Prince Street), an eyeglass boutique, meanwhile pursues a sweet theme: "Luxe lenses are sold right next to Italian hard candies, luscious lollipops, English jams and teas, and hair-raising espresso drinks at the Cacao Bar." All of this works quite nicely for these stores, Mr. Underhill notes, "because by positioning themselves as multiple destinations, they are generating more traffic."

E-Choupals. (6/5/03). The term is based on "the Hindi word for gathering place," and it is at the center of an e-commerce trend now sweeping four states in rural India, as reported by Cris Prystay in *The Wall Street Journal.* Creating this wave is a company called ITC Ltd., "one of India's major agricultural trading houses," which so far "has set up 2,100 computer kiosks in private homes," which the locals use not only to get the best prices for their crops, but to use the profits to buy everything from dry goods to insurance to televisions and even automobiles. Kids use the connectivity to help complete their homework assignments, too.

"The ultimate objective is to increase the productivity of the village," says Ram Kumar of ITC, which is 30 percent owned by British American Tobacco. Of course, another objective—for ITC and other multinationals including Hyundai, and Philips Electronics—is to tap into the largely untapped rural markets.

"Urban India is getting saturated," says K. Ramachandran, CEO of Philips in India. "In the cities, everyone who can afford a television set has one. If you want to maintain high growth, you have to penetrate into rural India."

Companies like Hyundai employ certain village "opinion leaders," to help things along. One such buzzmaker is Buta Singh, the "village headman" in Kaler, in northeastern Punjab, population 300. "If I tell them I like a particular brand," says Mr. Singh, "they'll go out and get it."

For ITC, the e-choupal strategy has resulted in some $200 million in sales of "products such as seeds and fertilizers" to villages last year. The company also now purchases "about 25 percent of its commodities, valued at about $50 million" via the e-choupals, each of which costs $3,400 to install. ITC, www.itcportal.com, is currently "adding five more e-choupals a day…and ultimately plans to wire up 100,000 villages," giving "it potential access to 10 million consumers." The company also hopes to sell its data on "the consumption habits of rural India" to other companies.

Retail Lit. (6/17/03). Books and magazines—not circulars or discounts—are the trendiest trend in retail merchandising, as reported by *USA Today*'s Lorrie Grant. Bloomingdale's is sending its 270,000 loyalty program members a "130-page glossy magazine," called *B*, "highlighting fashion, travel destinations, entertaining and celebrity profiles." Everyone else can buy it for $3.95 a copy, or else subscribe.

Limited Too plans to sell special editions of Julia Devillers' series of books, www.girlwise.com, "about the lives of four best friends," which happens to include "generic fashion references throughout." Coach, meanwhile, has published an 80-page, $18.95 beauty that basically glorifies its "handbags, hats, shoes and other products," available at its store as well as in bookstores.

Thing is, none of these publications include toll-free numbers, website addresses—or much of anything that directly push a sale. Instead, it's all about building the brand image. In a recession. Go figure. "These customers want to be in the know, and we're credible to them," explains Frank Berman, marketing chief at Bloomingdale's.

"Entertainment is a very important factor in a girl's life, so we have taken our brand into that," says Scott Bracale, head of catalog and online marketing at Limited Too. "We did it in collaboration with our 60th anniversary to show the history of one place and communicate it to people interested in the brand," chimes in Reed Krakoff, president and chief creative officer of Coach.

Marketing gurus also offer their take. "Consumers want to use the lifestyle books to inform themselves," says Cynthia Cohen of Strategic Mindshare, a retail-consulting firm. Others cite the book-and-magazines approach as a way to help "retailers to save on skyrocketing advertising costs because they can be more strategic." They can "keep older styles in front of customers," for example.

William Cody of Wharton's Jay H. Baker Retailing Initiative meanwhile sees something other than subtlety in the approach. "The rule of thumb is to scream louder and longer in your advertising," he says. "And this gives you another voice to make the lifestyle aspirational"

Salons v. Cancer. (11/6/03). Arthur Ashe was a great tennis player, but his greatest legacy may well turn out to be the communications innovations of The Arthur Ashe Institute of Urban Health, suggests a *New York Times* article by Richard Perez-Pena.

The challenge is, because African-Americans "have so much mistrust in the health system...the usual outreach doesn't work," explains Ruth C.

Browne, the Institute's executive director. As a result, more black women die of breast cancer—even though they don't get the disease any more often than white women, according to Dr. Marilyn White.

The Institute's solution is really clever. It is grounded in the simple insight that neighborhood beauty salons are "part social club, part counseling center, part bulletin board...a place where women can air their concerns away from men." And so the Institute has recruited "about 25" salon owners as breast cancer educators. At Michou Hair in East Flatbush, for example, Micheline Eduoard explains how to do a self-exam, and advises regular mammograms, in between the cuts and the curls.

Most customers are grateful for this, although a few become "angry that you brought it up," says Jo Ann Mosely of Dermalax, another participating salon. But all in all, the approach is not only effective, it is in keeping with something Arthur Ashe himself once said: "Start where you are. Use what you have. Do what you can."

The Institute also brings its health education campaign to "public libraries and tattoo and piercing parlors." The Institute's "next project will have barbers talk to men about prostate cancer." Arthur Ashe founded the Institute in late December 1992, just two months before his own death from AIDS.

Atmospherics

Behavioral Designer. (1/31/03). His name is F. Michael Graves and he says, "I'm the first fresh idea in auto retailing in 70 years," as reported by Phil Patton in *The New York Times*. No, not *that* Michael Graves (note the upfront "F"). *This* Michael Graves, of Dallas, Texas, is the one who created the King's Tour for Priscilla and Lisa Marie at Graceland, and is turning the same kind of magic at a place called "Planet Ford, a $12 million, 32-acre complex that may well be the epitome of the new dealership style.

At Planet Ford, a huge globe rises from a reflecting pool, and employees in golf carts greet arriving customers with bottled water. Inside, service department teams wear uniforms like those on Nascar pit crews, and buyers are handed the keys to their new cars amid flashing lights and noisy sound effects."

Graves calls this "autotainment" and has also applied the concept to Planet Dodge, where the effect is created with a kind of "Ritz-Carlton treatment," with a concierge greeting customers by name. Not to be confused with Planet Honda, created by a different god of design. Planet Honda is the blue-hued satellite in this emerging solar system. Yes, hundreds of Honda dealerships nationwide are now bathed in a "bright, almost electric" blue, intended to "catch the eye of the passing motorist as quickly as the distinctive look and logos of McDonald's, the Gap or Exxon…"

Inside the $4.5 Planet Honda in Clifton, New Jersey, customers are treated to "soothing New Age music and a fragrance devised by an aromatherapist…described as 'a proprietary blend of essential oils that create a sense of abundance and joy'…There are a coffee bar, a large video screen on a wall and a children's play area with books and plastic toys."

The automotive shopping experience at Manhattan Auto Group meanwhile includes a rock-climbing wall near the Ford trucks, and a track on the roof where prospective buyers can test-drive a Land Rover on cobble-stones. The Fletcher Jones Lexus dealership in Las Vegas offers masseurs manicurists, and a wireless network. "In today's society," says manager Bob McCrary, "people don't want to just sit around watching *The Price is Right.*" Or, as Volkswagen CEO Gerd Klaus explains it: "You can't sell a luxury car in a dump." The new Volkswagen look, designed by Gensler and Palladia, is "based on a European market square."

Coney Island Cool. (2/5/03). When some people went to the Hamp-tons, others would walk the Boardwalk, says Arlene Simon, who is today celebrating yesterday's "landmark" designation of Coney Island's long-defunct Child's Restaurant, as reported by Diane Cardwell in *The New York Times.* Even for those who didn't grow up with it, Childs should ring significant—it "pioneered the self-service cafeteria," the forerunner of the fast-food restaurant.

In its day, Childs was "a community hub where older people could eat, teenagers could go to get away from their parents and children could learn how to eat out." Historian Jeffrey Kroessler says Childs "had a civilizing influence." It was an "icon of elegance and quality at reasonable prices."

Today, it sits there, just locked up, fading away, a shell of its former self. But it oozes *wabi-sabi.* Built in 1923, it combines "elements of Spanish Colonial Revival…'with numerous maritime allusions that refer to its sea-side location.'" Its facade is "festooned with elaborate, terra cotta nautical motifs, including Neptune rising from the sea draped in seaweed, Euro-pean ships and intricate crustaceans and other sea creatures." Says one who remembers its heyday: "It really evokes an era that is really so much pass-ing into literature and film."

Inside, Childs was "outfitted with white tiled walls and floors and white marble countertops, and the employees dressed in starched white uniforms to convey a sense of cleanliness…" Some recall it was also a whites-only establishment, at times. Still, Childs grew into one of America's largest res-taurant chains, but eventually was acquired and the brand disappeared. It is now seen as a linchpin of a Coney Island re-development, perched as it is "about a block west of the Brooklyn Cyclones' minor-league baseball stadium.

Just how the building will be used is an open question, although turning it into catering hall or a restaurant appears to be under consideration. Says one supporter: "We just can't go knocking things down. It brings back the days when people used to go to Coney Island and enjoy themselves."

HoJo's Mojo. (2/19/03). As recently as the 1970s, Howard Johnson's was a 500-restaurant chain, but today it boasts just eleven, reports food critic William Grimes in the *New York Times*. Howard Johnson's—HoJo's—in its heyday, had sales exceeding those of McDonald's, Burger King and KFC combined. Heck, it was scooping its own brand of high-butterfat ice cream in 28 flavors before Haagen-Dazs was so much as a gleam in Ben & Jerry's eyes. Why, there were three HoJo's in New York's Times Square theater district alone!

Now, there is but one—and it is rumored to be nearing the end of its more than 40-year run (a rumor that was news to Franchise Associates, "the company that licenses the now puny Howard Johnson's, restaurant chain").

Into the orange glow of that landmark spot, at 46th & Broadway, ventured critic Grimes. Here's what he saw: "Row upon row of brownish-orange leather booths stretched to the horizon line, all wrapped around vintage Formica tables. On the right, an ancient soda fountain dispensed the famous ice creams. At the back was a bar, decorated with an illuminated ad for Miller High Life beer featuring a curvy blonde with a flipped-up hairdo and heavy eyeliner. It seemed to date from the mid-1960's, like the faded Broadway posters for shows like *Hallelujah, Baby*.

The wait staff, Grimes relays, "carry on the great tradition of gum-snapping, hand-on-waist Brooklyn waitresses," who "radiate warmth" and "validate your choices." They tend to be from Eastern Europe or the West Indies, and do not appear to be aspiring actresses. No J.Lo's at HoJo's.

The food, well, apparently it's pretty much a far piece from the days when the original Mr. Howard Johnson obsessed over cleanliness and food quality back in the 1950s. Comedian Penn Jillette, who haunts the Times Square HoJo's "with assorted friends and misfits each Friday night at 10:30" comments: "The fried food at HoJo's is a good bet, because you know they've had the deep fryers running for a while, and you get the extra flavor of the previous meal."

There's also that $3.25 martini, the mac-and-cheese and the HoJo Cola. So, whatever happened to HoJo's? Grimes explains that "other operations picked up on the HoJo's formula and did the same thing, only cheaper, or with a more contemporary twist." For nostalgists, pop culturists and marketing strategists, HoJo's mojo is chronicled and celebrated at Web sites including www.autoage.org and www.hojoland.com

Hotel Majarajah. (2/21/03). The Indian government hasn't recognized its former rulers for decades, but "celebrity-crazy" tourists are drawn to former palaces as hotels and deposed leaders as hosts, reports Karen Mazurkewich in *The Wall Street Journal.* "The maharaja name sells," says Narendra Singh, son-in-law of the Maharaja Sawai Singh of Jaipur, and manager of the City Palace hotel there. The Maharaja himself hosts "corporate-incentive nights" at his old home, making "small talk" with his guests as he "sits regally at his crystal dining table." The evening's festivities also include "an elephant salute, rose-petal confetti, a seductive performance by Jaipur's favorite dancer and a fireworks display."

But the real draw is the Maharaja himself: "He creates atmosphere," says one satisfied guest. Oh, it's a long jaunt from the days of "tiger hunts" and "royal parties for the likes of Eleanor Roosevelt and the future Queen Elizabeth II." Actually, it was the current Maharaja's father who first turned a palace into a hotel, leasing the family's Rambagh Palace in 1972 to the Taj Group. The family has since re-claimed control of the property, and son-in-law Singh "believes he can elevate the family's fortunes to heights rarely seen since…1931," the year his father-in-law was born.

Tourism professionals tend to confirm the potential. Dutch tour operator Yvonne van Mierlo comments: "We've stayed in all the five-star hotels in India, but the heritage properties—like this one—have more of a personal touch." Other properties include the Umaid Bhawan Palace in Jodhpur, said to offer "an Arabian nights kind of adventure," and "still served by some of its original staff."

The Maharana of Udaipur, meanwhile, has invested some $10 million to restore "his City Palace in Udaipur and now operates nine hotels, is developing four more and is in talks on buying at least another two." His properties host "film shoots, business convention, weddings, and even…male beauty contests." Of his critics he says: "They are maharajas, and I am a businessman."

Hotel California. (2/21/03). "There's a place where legend becomes reality, and this one has taken on a life of its own," says John Stewart, co-owner of the newly renovated Hotel California in Todos Santos, Mexico, as quoted by *USA Today*'s Laura Bly.

With visions of "dark desert highways" and "pink champagne on ice" dancing in his head, Stewart and partner Witold Twardowski paid $950,000 for the former $2.50-a-night backpacker "flophouse" that is said to be the inspiration for the 1976 Eagles album, *Hotel California*, that "sold more than 16 million copies" and "won a best-record Grammy." The single hit number one for a week, in 1997.

When the refurbished Hotel California re-opens as a hotel next month, after a half a million in renovations, rooms will run $225 per night, and a yuppiefied bar will pour the cervezas as it plays the famous Eagles tune for anyone who has to hear it. Any connection between that song and this hotel is tenuous, at best, however. A spokesperson for the Eagles says no such link exists and that the song was not written there, as legend has it. Investor Twardowski basically says he couldn't care less, that there's "a magic and an energy in this town that goes way beyond whether it was written here or not."

About that, he's probably right. Todos Santos has been building momentum as an "artist community" since the early 1980s, having attracted "an eclectic cadre of artists, Hollywood creative types and surfers willing to drive a mile or more on unmarked, teeth-rattling roads to reach beaches where pelicans often outnumber boards…" Its remoteness seems to be the key to its attractiveness, an allure that some suggest has been fed by a post-9/11 desire to hide away.

Though the place reportedly remains a bit dog-infested and crime-ridden, "a Mexico City developer recently paid nearly $4 million for an oceanfront stretch that will host the area's first golf course, resort hotel and timeshares—or so the scuttlebutt goes." In the meantime, tourist information can be had at todossantos-baja.com

Cool Motels. (3/30/03). The golfers and blue-haired ladies still flock to Palm Springs, and the "ticky-tacky tourist shops" haven't gone away, reports Janelle Brown in *The New York Times*. However, behind high gates, the young, the rich and the beautiful are once again taking mineral baths at "modernist havens" such as the Sagewater Spa. "Young people who care about design" are said to be into it, too—that is, a "mid-century modernist revival" of "run-down" motels.

These motels are small. The Desert Star offers just four rooms, while the Sagewater has only seven. That adds to the air of exclusivity, to be sure, as does the attention to authenticity: "At the Orbit In downtown Palm Springs, for example, each room is named after—and filled with furniture by—a modernist designer."

The Desert Star is decked out with "Eames side tables and George Nelson bubble lamps and thick white shag rugs." The hotels share a similar 1950s blueprint of "U-shaped buildings surrounding a courtyard with a pool, hidden from the street by tall gates." Steve Samiof, owner of the Desert Star, "calls his aesthetic, 'store-front modern.'"

Achieving that aesthetic doesn't come easily. "You should have seen this place when we bought it," says Rhoni Epstein, owner of the Sagewater Spa, built in 1954. "There was no roof, just two plywood boards. There was tar on the floors, sand on the deck, a leak in the gas line. We had to rip out the pool and retile it."

Now it's "all pristine white and cool green." Guests cook in their own kitchens, enjoy cocktails on the patio and hopefully play well with the other guests, "(at hotels this small, there is no avoiding the other guests)."

Says Ms. Epstein: "We really wanted our own particular brand of hospitality. It feels happy here, and there's something really cozy."

Pudding Parlor. (4/2/03). Rice to Riches is the name of a just-opened store on Spring Street in NYC's Little Italy, and rice pudding is the only item sold, as reported by Fred A. Bernstein in *The New York Times*. "Everyone loves rice pudding," says Peter Moceo, proprietor. He and his chef—Jemal Edwards—are hard at work whipping up 18 flavors of rice pudding with wild names like Coffee Collapse, Sesame Survivor and Chocolate Cherry Crime Scene. "I spent a lot of time," Mr. Moceo says, "looking for words that would go together."

Peter-the-rice-man also spent a lot of money creating a retail experience to match his concept. Rice to Riches transports its patrons with a glass portal shaped like a grain of rice. The shop's "space-agey" interior is of "orange and white Lucite," while the plastic dishes are in colors that match the flavors. On the wall hangs a flat screen television showing videos of Mr. Moceo's white Maltese. Originally, the idea was that his dog would battle "larger dogs for rice pudding prizes" but that didn't work out.

The counter—it's shaped like a grain of rice, too. What, exactly, is this guy thinking? Originally, he was thinking he'd "open a sit-down restaurant featuring only rice dishes." Then, on a trip to Italy, the pudding idea germinated while he was eating "intensely flavored desserts in Florence's stylish gelaterias."

Back home, it was a bit of a challenge getting a landlord to rent space for a pudding parlor (most didn't think anyone could make any money at this). Even more challenging was coming up with recipes that worked (rice is not the most cooperative starchy, edible seed on the planet). Sesame Survivor, for example, includes "light brown sugar, dark brown sugar and Joyva tahini paste."

Other flavors include pineapple-basil and pistachio-sage. The flavorings tend to be expensive and the rice is strictly of the "firm-grained sushi" variety. An eight-ounce serving goes for $4.50, and for an extra 25 cents, you can add various exotic toppings, like port-soaked currants. Mr. Moceo says he plans to open four more stores in Manhattan, and to build a larger kitchen so he can supply his puddings to restaurants.

Delta's Divas. (4/11/03). She is a "bargain-hunting, yet sophisticated woman, age 35 to 54," and the bull's-eye target of a low-cost airline called Song, brought to you by Delta, reports Nicole Harris in *The Wall Street Journal.*

That deal-seeking woman is tagged by Delta as the "discount diva" and the airline thinks it has her number with Song, which "is scheduled to take flight next week, with plans for almost 150 daily flights serving the Northeast and Florida." Song's strategy is based on research showing that "women do 90 percent of all online research into leisure travel and make 75 percent of leisure-travel decisions."

The husband may be the head of the household but the woman is the neck, right? (That's from *Greek Wedding*). The idea, based on the insight, is to offer the divas "style and choice." The execution, based on the idea, includes "sky-blue leather seats...Pizzeria Uno sandwiches, Cinnabon coffee cakes and organic meals designed by Chef Michel Nischan" of "W" hotel fame.

Song will also have a "digital television at every seat...as well as pay-per-view movies, Internet surfing and stored music that users can mix into customized play lists." The kids will have use of Nintendo Gameboys and flight attendants will also sell earplugs and eyeshades (presumably for the men).

All of this is "meant to attract the wives, girlfriends and female colleagues of the men buying tickets on other carriers." John Lister of Lister Butler thinks this could work: "These women are probably into seeking out a higher quality of experience for their families than the man in the house, who might not be willing to spend his time looking for it."

Gary Stibel of New England Consulting thinks it might *not* work: "If you've got a dozen different value propositions," he says, "you end up getting none of them right and therefore disappoint many or most of your customers." He also said that he doesn't think any one consumer group is big enough "to make any airline sing." (Somebody please buy him a C-Sharp).

And about that unusual brand name—Song, www.flysong.com—John Selvaggio, who heads the new airline explains: "Everybody knows a song, everyone likes a song."

The Georgetown Saloon. (4/18/03). Sitting in the dark, on a narrow one-way street, a tight left turn after a hairpin right, the Georgetown Saloon (near Wilton, Connecticut) is a little cracker box of a joint. Time may have forgotten this place, with its rough-hewn decor, the old cowboy rifles and bleached bones of various prairie dwellers now taking up permanent residence on pine-paneled walls.

But on a Thursday night—every Thursday night—the place is jam-packed and rocking with mostly older and mostly white guys, playing mostly the blues, that most of them mostly play from behind their bedroom doors, most probably.

Thursday, you see, is Open Mic Night at the Georgetown Saloon, and the experience just reeks of authenticity, of players who play for the love of playing, and don't much care that time and fashion has passed them by. They line up, their Strats and Teles strapped around their necks, each waiting his turn for a moment on the tiniest of stages, to play songs both familiar and obscure, some hot and some not.

The night is hosted by a band that's otherwise known as The Twinkies (now there's a sponsorship opportunity for you), which has been gigging non-stop at the Saloon for many, many years. It's got to be 20 years, at least. Could it be 30 years now?

The Twinkies are led by Tom Schulz, a former *Hee-Haw* cast member, and Chance Browne, the cartoonist of *Hi & Lois* fame. Their bass player, Kenny Owens, sometimes works with Joe Cocker and Jose Feliciano (who has been known to sit in on this Thursday tradition now and again).

I was there to see Jon Manners, www.jonmanners.com, my big brother, in from Minnesota, who bravely strapped on an acoustic guitar of his own making and, accompanied only by a drummer, turned in a gripping, stellar performance of tunes from his latest CD, *Frankie Said.*

Open Mic Night at the Georgetown Saloon—Yanni, it isn't. Actually, it's kind of like American Idol, but in reverse. No illusions of fame or fortune (then again, Keith Richards has played this Saloon). No rude judges…just a crowd that hoots and whistles after every song. No trendy bartenders or beautiful people, just real players playing real instruments, and remembering what that was like. Total cost of the evening: $6.24.

The Ice Bar. (6/2/03). The hottest spot in Stockholm is a nightclub where the temperatures hover at about 23F and the patrons are handed parkas, mittens and boots at the door, reports Julia Keller in *The Chicago Tribune*.

The Ice Bar, as it is called, is tucked into a corner of Stockholm's Nordic Sea Hotel. The walls outside are of glass, but inside the place is "constructed entirely of ice, from the infrastructure—walls, ceilings, tables, bars—to the accoutrements: Drinks arrive in glasses made of ice," and "ice sculptures are the only decor." It is attracting trendies with its "atmospherics and a perversely appealing physical discomfort."

"We get people from everywhere," says host Elin Alvemark, adding: "Ninety-nine percent of the time, they say, 'Oh, my God!'" As Ms. Keller describes it: "The Ice Bar combines a cool, almost ethereal beauty—all that crystalline context—with the sci-fi, high-tech feel of an alien latitude." It holds just 30 people, but harbors no end of jokes about ice. "It's, 'Hey, can I have some more ice cubes in my drink?'" says bartender Juan Gonzales, who says he acts as though he hasn't heard that one before.

The Ice Bar actually follows in the footsteps of Jukkasjavi's Ice Hotel, www.icehotel.com, located in the "Lapland region above the Arctic Circle." Carved each winter by artists, The Ice Hotel is a 50-room inn where travelers have chilled at 5 below since 1989—that is, until spring arrives and the place melts.

Such a fate does not appear to be in store for The Ice Bar, however, which may be coming soon to a block near you. Plans are to expand to locations in other parts of the world, including the United States." The venture is co-sponsored, cleverly, by Absolut vodka.

Casual Exotica. (6/4/03). "Mass-produced restaurants can be an interesting novelty," reports Marian Burros of *The New York Times*, explaining the surprising appeal of Applebee's, Outback and The Olive Garden in big, bad Manhattan. A touch of blandness actually seems to be just the ticket for certain New Yorkers, who routinely pass up the quality—and quirks—offered up by NYC's many good, little, neighborhood eateries.

"It's a little bit of the suburbs that you can't get here," says Leja Kress, a hip, young New Yorker, explaining her presence at the Applebee's in Battery Park City. She adds: "This place cracks us up. All the fake memorabilia. It's like trying to look like it's old, but it's only been here for a year."

Irony aside, other dining sophisticates say they like the consistency and convenience of a nationally branded restaurant. "Here, you know how it's going to be," says one such diner. Still others note the "comfort" effect: "I'm from a small town in Michigan and it reminds me of home," says Amanda Keckonen, a marketing professional who likes The Olive Garden. Restaurant consultant Clark Wolf, meanwhile, says the popularity of casual chains exposes New Yorkers for what they really are: "New Yorkers as a group are not at the cutting edge and that's the dirty secret," he says.

Somewhat less of a secret is the money the chains spend to attract customers, and then to make sure their dining experience is both fast and friendly. Zane Tankel, chairman of Apple-Metro, owner of the 22 Applebee's in metro NYC, pegs the marketing budget at $100 million. All told, Applebee's Outback and Olive Garden spend about $350 million a year on marketing, according to stock analyst Andrew Barish.

In addition to a constant buzz of TV commercials, the deep pockets also buy waitstaffs that are "overarchingly friendly." At Outback, the help is trained to sit down with customers if there's an open seat, and at Red Lobster, they kneel down, so they're at eye-level with the patrons. Maybe most telling of all, NYC's casual diners don't make the choice because it is cheaper—an informal survey found that a casual-dining bill typically is about the same as it would be just about anywhere else in the neighborhood.

Whirlpool's Insperience. (6/12/03). It's not a store, mind you, it's a *studio*, as reported by Scott Kirsner in *Fast Company* (Jul 03). It's an experiment, actually, but one that Whirlpool's David Provost, whose title is "director of purchase experience," hopes will transform retail. It is certainly something different. Whirlpool's Insperience Studio, inspeiencestudio.com, situated in Atlanta's Buckhead area since last November, invites shoppers to "bring their chores with them." Some potential customers do their laundry there, while others try baking bread or cookies: "One man brought in a bag of trash to crunch in the compactor."

The idea was that of one Scott Phillips, and it not only overcomes the traditional "sea of white" boxes for which appliance stores are known and loathed, but also sets up a veritable laboratory for new product development and studying "how consumers interact with appliances." It's a "boot camp for salespeople," too. It is even possible to throw a holiday or birthday party there. It is not a "free ride" for consumers, however. If you plan to show up, expect a 90-minute tour with a "selection consultant," who will walk you through a "series of kitchen, patio, and laundry-room 'vignettes.'" Every kitchen tells a story.

To make sure he can prove the concept's worth to Whirlpool, Mr. Phillips has "developed a list of metrics" intended to quantify its payoff. These include foot traffic, market share in Atlanta, number of builders as new customers, as well as "sales figures at retailers whose salespeople are trained at Insperience."

The salespeople—er, selection consultants—"also follow up with consumers who have visited Insperience to see whether they need any more information—and find out which appliances they decided to buy." Results will be reviewed on the concept's first anniversary, this November, which apparently will determine its future. "We're fighting every day to show that this is a great investment for Whirlpool," says Provost," adding, "There's a lot of pressure."

Bookless Bookstore. (6/23/03). A funny thing happened when the New Words Bookstore closed. Customers kept coming—just not for books, as reported by Julie Flaherty in *The New York Times*. What keeps the customers coming are *events*—author appearances, writer's workshops and open-mic readings. "We're well past saying we have to fight the chains, or we have to fight the Internet," says Gilda Bruckman, one of the store's founders. "Obviously if it's possible to buy books much less expensively, that's not the area to compete."

That bit of insight actually was based on a $75,000 research study, thanks to a grant from The Ford Foundation. The study found "that people would come in from the suburbs to see a popular author, but not just to buy a book." And so it was concluded, "that access and connection could be as important as bookselling."

What makes all of this especially interesting is the New Words is a women's bookstore, founded in 1974 in a single room of a Victorian house in Cambridge, Massachusetts. It was very much a niche business, "promoting and selling little-known books from women's presses," and "stocking pamphlets on subjects related to women."

However, with many other women's bookstores, New Words fell prey to its own success, "as the authors they promoted went mainstream." When Amazon.com and the megastores moved in, well, that was all she wrote. "Our interest is really in words, ideas, writing and expression," says Ms. Bruckman, explaining the new focus. Comments Ann Christopherson, president of the American Bookseller's Association: "There are ways to expand the market by changing your identity a bit without losing what you started out to do."

In the case of New Words, that includes not making much money. "No one ever saw this as an investment except emotionally," says Ms. Bruckman. New Words is currently raising money for a re-launch as a not-for-profit center. In the meantime, it continues to promote its events on its website: www.newwordsbooks.com.

Lucky Strike Lanes. (7/15/03). It is a bowling alley, yes, but it is being hyped and hugged as a hip Hollywood hangout, reports Ann Oldenburg in *USA Today*. It is Lucky Strike Lanes, bowlluckystrike.com, and its "upscale, retro lounge feel" is being whispered the same breathless breath as Ian Schrager's Sky Bar in the Mondrian Hotel, www.mondrianhotel.com.

"I love bowling!" endorses Kelly Osbourne, one of the many young popsters who attended the venue's opening party. "It is so much better than being at a club—clubs are so generic and predictable most of the time," she adds.

At Lucky Strike, it is all "floor-to-ceiling screens," projecting "everything from great works of art to cartoons. There's a private party room and a 35-foot bar made out of Lane 16 from the legendary Hollywood Star Lanes, which was closed last August. And instead of those hard vinyl seats...Lucky Strike has comfy sofas."

And celebrities—oh, does it have celebrities. Justin Timberlake, Cameron Diaz, Fred Durst, Christina Aguilera, Robin Williams and Danny Masterson, for instance. They all attended the "15 Hottest Stars Under 25" party, hosted by *Teen People* at Lucky Strike last May.

Dining choices include classic bowling alley items like hot dogs, hamburgers and pizza, but a 60-seat restaurant also serves "dishes such as scallop skewers, mixed baby greens and lemon-berry meringue tart." The kitchen is run by Along Came Mary, www.alongcamemary.com, caterers of the Jennifer Aniston-Brad Pitt wedding.

Lucky Strike is the brainchild of Gillian and Steven Foster, who have created "various entertainment and dining complexes in more than 20 states," and plan "to open more Lucky Strike Lanes in Orange County, Boston and Toronto." Look out, miniature golf.

Asheville, NC. (10/3/03). It is in the Appalachian Mountains and over the last five years it has "morphed into one of the South's hippest hangouts," reports Gene Sloan in *USA Today*. "Anytime you can get bluegrass music and burlesque in the same town, you know you're in an interesting place," says Kim MacQueen, a Seattle expat who opened Gold Hill Espresso and Fine Teas, the first of the downtown Asheville's many coffee shops, eight years ago.

Today, "there are 10 espresso bars within a short walk" downtown. In between the caffeine it's all music clubs, vegetarian restaurants, galleries, organic markets, mom-and-pop boutiques, tattoo parlors and earth-friendly stores. Some call it America's new "counterculture capital," or "the Santa Fe of the East."

All of that in this "mountain outpost" of 77,000 residents that didn't pay off its depression-era debt until 1976, in a region better known for Billy Graham and religious conservatism. So, how did it all happen? Asheville's transformation from ghost town to hipster haven began, legend has it, more than ten years ago when a fellow named John Cram opened a gallery called Blue Spiral 1, there. Some folks thought he was crazy, but others followed his lead, and "by the late '90s, the downtown was starting to thrive."

Okay, so that's what happened. *Why* it happened is the real story here. The region actually has long been home to creative types, many of whom first arrived "more than a century ago to work on George Vanderbilt's monumental Biltmore Estate." When the job was done, the artisans stayed, making "the area the epicenter of the American craft movement for a century." In addition, "the region's beauty and isolation lured a flock of big-name Bauhaus artists fleeing Nazi Germany, including Josef Albers, who created an artist's colony at nearby Black Mountain College."

The Biltmore Estate, meanwhile, has always made the town a tourist attraction—and all the moreso as tourists have tended to avoid major destinations ever since you-know-what. So happening is this town that some locals are worried it will begin to "attract the cookie-cutter chain stores that so far have stayed away." Others are more sanguine. Says John Cram of Blue Spiral 1: "I'm looking forward to the day they start calling Santa Fe the Asheville of the West."

Merchants Square. (4/2/03). Tourism may be down in Colonial Williamsburg, but retailing is up—way up, reports Maureen Milford in *The New York Times*. Indeed, the number of admission tickets sold last year to the 30-acre outdoor history museum—840,000—is the lowest tally since 1969. However, annual sales per square foot at Colonial Williamsburg's 40 shops known as Merchants Square—$500 to $600—is about double that of the average enclosed mall, as documented by the International Council of Shopping Centers.

So, while Talbot's and Chico's may not be exactly what Colonial Williamsburg's founders had in mind, the merchandising possibilities actually have been in play since 1932, when "John D. Rockefeller Jr. established a retail district to serve residents and visitors at the restored former capital of Virginia." It's hoped that the arrival of women's specialty chains "should appeal to the growing number of retirees in the Williamsburg area." Accordingly, Merchants Square is about to expand with an additional "34,000 square feet of shops...at the corner of Duke and Gloucester and North Boundary Streets."

The museum's directors, naturally, are taking care that the expansion does not in any way conflict with the Colonial Williamsburg experience, which is famous for its "staff members in period costume demonstrating how life was lived more than two centuries ago." Comments Edward H. Able, Jr. of the American Association of Museums: "A cigarette outlet or a liquor store or a topless bar is not something people would expect a public trust institution to be engaged in, even if they're just leasing the space."

The developers are also taking great care from an architectural standpoint, with the new structure consisting of four buildings, each of which will look as though built at different times. Pretty cool. The new stores are slated to open in November, and the rent per square foot—$45—seems a modest premium relative to the $30 to $35 commanded by the typical strip mall.

The Buyer's Club. (7/16/03). "He is all about the miracle of growing things," says a customer of "Tovey Halleck, an artist and farmer," who "grows produce at his farm" in the Catskills, and then sells it from a "studio storefront" on New York City's Lower East Side, as reported by Andrea Strong in *The New York Times*.

Yep, right there on the sidewalk, amid his "twisted wrought-iron sculptures of trees and plants," on Avenue B, between 12th and 13th Streets, you can find Tovey "in a tattered, dirty T-shirt and beat-up jeans," trading in vegetables that some would say also qualify as works of art.

He yanks his veggies from the ground and drives them down to the East Village from his farm each Wednesday morning, June to November, and sets up shop from 4 to 9 p.m. "A late-afternoon market is perfect for the East Village," he says. "We get up later than the rest of the city."

His vegetables—"newly uprooted garlic, onions and chives," as well as "rose-tinged rhubarb…jade-color dandelion greens…heirloom tomatoes the colors of a blazing sunset"—are grown on his 12-acre farm in Roxbury, New York. "His farmhands are members of the *Witnesses*, an East Village progressive-rock band, who work the land in exchange for using (Tovey's) barn to practice."

His customers are local chefs, some of whom change their menu based on whatever Mr. Halleck is picking. "I'll take everything he can give me," says Neil O'Malley of Rose Water, a Brooklyn restaurant. "If he says, 'I have dandelion greens, Jerusalem artichokes and turkey eggs,' that's what I'll cook."

Matt Reguin of 71 Clinton Fresh Food says that 45 to 50 percent of his menu comes from Tovey's farm stand, which he calls The Buyer's Club. No, it's not because he has a loyalty-card program. In fact, he invested in a scale only after a customer suggested it might make good business sense. His receipts tend to be written on "phone book covers or scraps of paper." Says customer Mary Cleaver of the Cleaver Company: "I like the purity of his approach."

Farmer's Markets. (8/1/03). As a concept, "it can apply to everything from street fairs with souvenirs and food carts to brick-and-mortar super-markets, like the prototypes just unveiled by natural-and-organic grocery Wild Oats," as explained by Nancy Keates in *The Wall Street Journal.*

In some cities, market inspectors make sure that "farmers are selling only what they grow," while at others, "those doing the selling aren't even farmers." Food regulations aside, "some markets are becoming almost cir-cus-like, thanks to attractions like blues bands, children's cooking classes and celebrity-chef demonstrations."

What really matters is, farmer's markets are going great guns. According to the U.S.D.A., the number of farmer's markets "has grown nine percent since 2000, to 3,100. Attendance has grown by "more than a third over four years, "with some cities reporting an increase of ten to twenty percent this year." This trend actually is traced back to the mid-1970s, "when chef Alice Waters started dishing out small-farm fare," in the hope that the market "would bring the community together by buying local goods from local growers."

These days, it seems the operative idea is more about copping "the latest status ingredients and face time with cult growers." Sharp elbows seem to have replaced *kumbaya*. "People have become really aggressive," says one shopper, who has taken to placing advance orders rather than fighting over the zucchini blossoms.

"It's become dog-eat-dog," says another shopper of the competition over limited greens. "I could hit them with my bag, but that wouldn't be nice." Some farmers manage nicely by raising prices—by as much as 30 percent. Few shoppers flinch. Some customers cope by plying their favorite farmers with home-baked cookies and dinners out. And one farmer brings the wisdom of Solomon to the table, cutting his last head of lettuce in half if a fight over it erupts. "It's only vegetables," he tells his customers. "Calm down."

The New Drive-Ins. (6/4/03). "If you love the movies and you love the outdoors, al fresco cinema really is kind of the best of both worlds," says film buff Chris Willman, as quoted by Claudia Puig in *USA Today*. "Movie theaters," he continues, "have traditionally been designed to take you away from the real world. But there's something interesting about seeing a movie screen integrated into an outdoor landscape. It's incongruous and fun, seeing these oversized images plopped down amid real life, as if the gods were paying an unexpected visit."

Mr. Willman is one of a number of growing fans of outdoor movie screenings—not at old-fashion drive-ins, but in settings such as a lake in San Antonio, where the audience watches from bobbing inner tubes...or from blow-up beds at the Rocky Mountain foothills. More than 100 major open-air theaters are said to be operating around America today, including one sponsored by Ikea, the furniture store chain, held weekly in Burbank, California. "People bring their own chairs and can hoot and holler at the screen where they cannot in a movie theater," comments Brian

Cobb, whose Way Out West Productions in Olympia, Washington, "has been showing movies outdoors for three years."

Perhaps the most intriguing manifestation of this trend is the twice-monthly event that's held both below—and above—the stars. The venue is the Hollywood Forever Cemetery, www.hollywoodforever.com, where about 1,500 people, including actor Jon Voight, devote a Saturday night to watching "classic films…projected on a marble mausoleum wall, near the graves of Douglas Fairbanks Jr. and Sr., Rudolph Valentino and Cecil B. De Mille.

Says one tentative attendee: "Being in a cemetery is a little freaky." Comments another: It's always really beautiful here…it's a great communal feeling." A third, meanwhile, enthuses: "If one were to believe in ghosts, it'd be fun to imagine some of the actors interred there coming out to watch themselves on screen."

Phish and the Bunny. (8/7/03). Phish, the improvisational rock band, is using the Bunny, an impermanent FM radio station, to add both entertainment and information to its giant music festivals, as reported by Seth Schiesel in a *New York Times* article (that is nearly as long as one of Phish's shows).

The article actually covers a whole range of ways in which Phish uses technologies "to create spectacular live concerts and phantasmagoric festival experiences that are more like computer-controlled theme parks than like the rock festivals of yesteryear." The show organizers make heavy use of walkie-talkies and wi-fi—and, of course, both lights and sound are courtesy of some really brainy technologies.

But the main thing is that when you draw some 60,000 Phish fans to what used to be Loring Air Force Base in remote, Limestone, Maine, you've created a city, and "it's vital to have a mass communication system." So Phish leased a 100,000-watt FM station for the event. The Bunny, as the band dubbed the station, not only served up "an eclectic mix of funk, rock, jazz, folk and electronic music," but also "simultaneously broadcast Phish's live sets." Imagine that—going to a live concert but listening to it on the radio.

Perhaps most important, The Bunny kept the concert-goers informed, and dispensed important safety advice, such as "Please do not ride on top of your vehicle."

No mention of whether this station had commercials or sponsors. Hm. A little too busy worrying about illegal downloads, perhaps? Meanwhile, elsewhere at this event, almost 2,000 CDs were burned by fans who lined up for up to two-and-a-half hours to enter The House of Live Phish, www.livephish.com, "a next-generation Internet cafe," created in collaboration with Apple: "Using one of 20 iMacs, concertgoers could not only surf the Web and send e-mail, they could also burn free custom CDs from the 154 live Phish tracks that were loaded on each computer."

Apple's hardware and software also were used by DJs to play music on the Bunny, although it was a "Windows laptop and Microsoft's Windows Media software" that put the station on the air. No sightings of Microsoft's legendary iLoo were reported at any time during the event, apparently.

Intangible Aesthetics. (8/14/03). It's the artists versus the engineers down in Texas, where a new E.P.A. code is forcing restaurateurs and other retailers to use ugly-but-efficient fluorescents instead of beautifully wasteful incandescent lights, as reported by Virginia Postrel in *The New York Times.*

At this point, the E.P.A. is simply encouraging states and cities to adopt the International Energy and Conservation Code. But for designers like Granville McAnear of Craig Roberts Associates in Dallas, it's a problem. "You have to have incandescent sources to be able to light the space nicely, softly—to get that warm feel, even in contemporary spaces," he says. Observes Ms Postrel: "For…any business that wants customers to feel special, lighting isn't just illumination anymore. It's identity, emotion and drama."

Actually, the point of the matter is not lighting so much as it is those many intangibles that create value in the hearts and minds of we consumers. As Ms. Postrel notes: "Cellphones do not just communicate; they let owners swap face plates and personalize rings. Toilet brushes do not just remove grime; they come in caddies with personality—from Phillippe Starck's sleek Excalibur to Stefano Giovannoni's playful Merdolino." Prices, she explains, "capture the relative value people put on intangibles," and reward "value you cannot easily count."

Just ask anyone in California politics about intangibles. But this is Texas, where notions of "tangible mechanical performance," as the economist Thorstein "Conspicuous Consumption" Veblen termed it in 1921, are giving the intangible types fits. "There is a significant difference between being able to see and being able to appreciate," says Fred Oberkircher, director of the center for lighting education at Texas Christian University.

Mark Rea, however, sees the issue in a different...light. "I can demonstrate through research that your color perception is better with fluorescent than it is with incandescent," he says. He's with Rensselaer Polytechnic Institute and says the designers don't know what they're talking about. Retorts Jan Martin, of Dallas design firm Zero 3: "I don't care what they say. Fluorescent is just not attractive."

Autonomedia's Sideshow. (8/25/03). A small, nonprofit, bookmobile-based publisher is bringing its utopian tomes to new audiences by treating them to an old-fashion, circus sideshow, reports Colin Moynihan in *The New York Times*. "It was really interesting," said one of the 30 curious folks who gathered in Brooklyn last Saturday night to watch a woman escape a straitjacket and lie on a bed of rusty nails, among other attractions. "And at the same time it was kind of creepy," she added.

This peculiar turn at event marketing is the brainchild of one Jim Fleming, who says he's been fascinated by bookmobiles since "the late 1960s, when he eagerly awaited a bookmobile carrying texts from university presses." He explains: "I could get books I couldn't find anywhere else." He dreamed up with the Bindlestiff Family Cirkus, www.bindlestiff.org, in the early 1990s, because "without the marketing budget enjoyed by the big houses," he knew he had to be "inventive to make his books available to a wide audience."

"Wide," in this case, is a relative concept. Autonomedia has published just north of 200 books, mostly in runs of about 3,000 copies each. Its best seller is a work called *Temporary Autonomous Zone*, by Hakim Bey, which has sold some 30,000 copies.

The bookmobile also features a "cabinet of curious information," a collection of "political pamphlets and the self-produced periodicals known as zines." Autonomedia's own offerings favor the "utopian and anti-authoritarian elements of philosophy. "So far, the sideshow is not breaking even. But Okra P. Dingle, one of its stars, says his main goal is to inspire his audiences. "If we dream alone," he says, "it's just a dream. But if we dream together, it's reality."

Billiards Bombshells. (10/13/03). Ewa Laurance and Jeanette Lee "are all the rage" on ESPN, reports Stephane Fitch in *Forbes*. They are also central to the growth of Brunswick Billiards, www.brunswick-billiards.com, whose president, John E. Stransky, recognizes how critical are women to sales of his company's billiards tables. Such purchases, his research found, are "male-initiated, wife-approved."

So that's "why Brunswick is now paying $1 million a year" to be the "table sponsor" of the Women's Professional Billiard Association's tournaments, www.wpba.com. It's not only that 400,000 people tune in to watch—it's also that 15 percent of them are women.

Brunswick's bet is that while the men tune in because Ewa and Jeanette are attractive, the women are also checking out those legs—that is, the table's legs. In recent years, the 158-year-old Brunswick Corp. has introduced "designer" tables with "wife appeal."

These include a model called The Manhattan, "a $15,000 steel-and-maplewood creation," that "can be customized with teal-colored felt." The company has also rolled out a line of "accessories and game-room packages that help design-conscious" women "trick out a game room."

Brunswick is also "pressing retailers to install fancy $100,000 displays," that Stransky calls "pavilions." These in-store environments "spotlight tables on polished hardwood floors, under flattering track lights and beamed cathedral ceilings." They are a far cry from pool table showrooms circa 1999, which used to follow the fluorescent-lit, stack 'em high school of merchandising.

"You wouldn't see pianos or dining tables stacked like that," says Stransky. So far, the feminine touch is working, as the designer items now account for "12 percent of Brunswick Billiard's sales," and overall sales "of pool tables and accessories rose 8.9 percent last year." Says Stransky: "Basically, we're in the furniture business."

Disney de Mexico. (10/12/03). It's not Disney, literally. But Xcaret (ISH-kuh-ray), a 200-acre theme park on Mexico's Mayan Riviera, creates a Disneyesque experience, reports Larry Bleiberg in *The Dallas Morning News*, The key difference, other than the Spanish accent, is that Xcaret extracts its thrills from nature. For example, rather than a "roller coaster, Xcaret's thrill ride is a 45-minute float on an underground river." And instead of Mickey Mouse, "the park uses its native turtles, flamingos and dolphins as its draw. But none of them is in costume—they're for real."

At Xcaret, www.xcaretcancun.com, tourists "enter through an informal museum with scale models of the region's Mayan ruins." There's an incubator where quail chicks hatch daily, an aquarium featuring a coral reef system, as well as open-air displays of all kinds of animals. "The park runs macaw, turtle and manatee conservation programs and has successfully bred dolphins in captivity."

The main attraction, however, is that 2,400-foot long underground river, which was "created by blasting out passageways and connecting sinkholes." Here, for the most part, the special effects are of the natural variety—roots dangle, the "green-blue" water glows and dances as it reflects the "sun and forms a kaleidoscopic reflection on the cave walls."

Xcaret has been around since 1990. It was created by Miguel Quintana, a Mexican-Hawaiian who originally purchased the land for himself, but persuaded owners of neighboring properties to turn the site into a tourist attraction after discovering "Mayan ruins and numerous sinkholes." The enterprise has grown to include gift shops, a 6,000-seat stadium and other Disney-like amenities. In fact, a hotel just opened on the property and other expansion ideas are in the works—including opening an additional park "in the Chiapas area of southern Mexico."

Plans to partner with Carnival Cruise lines to create a $2 million cruise port at Xcaret is, however, meeting some resistance from some locals, and is currently undergoing governmental review. In the meantime, a contingent from Disney's Epcot was spotted recently at Xcaret, and reportedly they were taking notes.

V.I.P. Voodoo. (10/17/03). "Voodoo is our culture," says Unik Ernst, who is from Haiti, as quoted by Lynda Richardson in *The New York Times.* Quickly, he adds: "We have good voodoo here, not the bad voodoo." He is talking about his new and very exclusive nightspot, called PM. It's located in New York's meatpacking district (natch) and the trappings include voodoo masks, bottles, dolls and paper mache heads of a horse and a cow.

Report is that the effect "evokes a forsaken gentlemen's club in Haiti circa the 1940s." No extra charge for the "throbbing" music and "impossibly tall and thin waitresses in Diane Von Furstenberg wiggling their hips" (assuming the bouncer lets you in, in the first place).

Unik (whose birth name was Franky, which he changed "because he likes to be unique") says he "sees the lounge as a kind of Haitian museum." He explains: "What we are doing is for our country. This is showing another side of Haiti. People think of Haitians as boat people, illiterate, that we are stupid, people who bring AIDS...We are intelligent and we have good ideas." It's not totally clear whether sending patrons to the second-floor bathroom if they are deemed insufficiently beautiful to use the one on the first floor is one of those good ideas.

It works for Unik, though, who certainly brought plenty of creative energy as well as a talent "for delivering desirable crowds to clubs" when he arrived in Miami with his family—including his brother and business partner, Kyky Conille, in 1990. He made his first splash in New York City with "a disco party to promote world peace," and later made a name for himself with his Wednesday night parties at the Serafina restaurant on Lafayette.

"I know what to do with the attention," says Unik. "I turn it into money." He says he now plans to turn into a PM franchise of hotels, resorts and Hollywood parties. "We are out there to show people a good time," he says, and later: "We don't get caught up in success. We know nothing is forever."

Cowgirl Creamery. (10/17/03). It is located inside the Tomales Bay Foods Store in Point Reyes Station, California, and it is where Peggy Smith and Sue Conley are leading a slow-motion revolution in American cheese, reports Jerry Shriver in *USA Today*.

If you knew Peggy and Sue, then you'd know they created a cheese called Red Hawk some four years ago. In August 2003, Red Hawk, priced at $18 a pound, "bested 615 other cheeses from 28 states and four countries to win Best of Show honors at the American Cheese Society's 20th Annual Conference in San Francisco."

"America," says Sue, "is on the precipice of tremendous change and development of our own cheese identity that is separate from Europe's. Soon, we'll refer to Red Hawk rather than Camembert." Red Hawk is a soft cheese, "triple-cream" and "washed-rind," in case that means something to you.

Actually, it's the washed-rind thing that's especially important. The cheese rinds are washed with brine water, which is said to "inhibit certain molds and promote the growth of *b.linens* during its six weeks of aging." That's what makes this cheese so stinking great. Also important is the Northern California climate—cool, humid and salty—that's perfect for aging cheese as well as for a long grazing season. Plus, Cowgirl's cows "aren't stressed by temperature extremes, and that affects the quality of the milk."

Cowgirl's customers get a great experience, too: We wanted an operation where people could see how the cheese was made—the grass, the cow, the farm," says Sue. "People can wander in and watch the cheesemaking through a window, and that lends a certain integrity to things…"

Part of that integrity is a commitment to small-scale production, meaning that Peggy and Sue plan not expansion for Cowgirl Creamery, but rather promotion of "small scale creameries" like theirs "in every town, in every region, so people wouldn't need to send for their cheese."

It's a trend that's already underway, as "the number of artisan cheese-makers has grown from a handful to more than 200 over the past decade," mostly in California, Wisconsin and New England, although "the South, which has lacked a cheese tradition, is emerging as a leader."

Olympic Beauty. (5/2/03). They're dressing 18th century statues of Greeks in 20th Century fashions by others at the Metropolitan Museum of Art, brought to you by Gucci and Conde Nast Publications, as reported by Herbert Muschamp in *The New York Times*.

The big idea is to mix-and-match modern gossamer with ancient Greece, and demonstrate "the unbroken line of classical influence," as described in the show's catalog. The even bigger idea is to enable Gucci's Tom Ford to insert his designs and fix an image within the realm of "contemporary classical" design.

The show is called "*Goddess*"—we're talking evening dresses here, and a "sensibility…rooted in 1930s Hollywood." As such, it is a "Depression-era mood," writes Muschamp, "an atmosphere oddly parallel to that of present-day America." Think "black and white and silver." Got it. "Fluidity," he meanwhile notes, "is a leading motif: a metaphor for women's freedom."

The show's "most authentically classical theme," however, is "the Greeks' passion for discovering unifying patterns in the world around them." As Muschamp explains: "Waves pass through hair, fabric and water. Greek art emphasized the similarity between them…This is what poetry meant to the Greeks: the art of weaving connective tissue."

He adds: "You'd think it would become tiresome to review the repetition of pleats, harness bodices, columnar sheaths and other standard devices. But discovering the infinite variations on these motifs is as untiring as watching waves break on the sand."

Lurking underneath it all, Muchamp observes, is "savagery and violence, the dark underside of classical restraint." The spring season, which "for the ancients was a time of violence, when new vegetation cracks the surface of the earth," provides a fitting metaphor for Muschamp, who comments: "It is difficult, now, for novelty to break through fashion's upper crust." The show runs through August 3rd.

Frank Lloyd Wretail. (10/29/03). "The distinctive ramp that dominates the room blocks sales representatives at their desks from seeing customers," writes Michael Luo in *The New York Times*. "The office space in the back is cramped," he continues. "And the…showroom itself can display only six cars, a problem when there are more than 40 different models…"

But, hey, it's okay, because this Mercedes-Benz showroom, built on Park Avenue at East 56th Street in Manhattan back in 1954 for Jaguar, was designed by Frank Lloyd Wright, "arguably the greatest American architect."

That explains the "twisting ramp" right in the middle, which is "a close relative to the six-story spiral that sprouts so brazenly some 30 blocks north," the Guggenheim Museum, guggenheim.org, also a Wright design. Despite the space's architectural pedigree, it came close to being gutted because of its ostensible impracticalities.

"Cars weren't lit properly because lighting fixtures were old and not performing well," says Randolph Gerner, the architect for the renovation. "They didn't have air-conditioning systems that functioned well." And so the dealership almost simply up and moved, leaving the space vulnerable to demolition.

Fortunately, this Mercedes dealership did the, uh, wright thing, and saw the design as an asset to its upscale merchandising aspirations. And so the light fixtures were improved, and various other repairs made in an effort some purists say falls short of a restoration, owing to certain liberties being taken with Frank's original specifications. "It's sympathetic, but it's not a restoration," says Kyle Johnson of the Frank Lloyd Wright Conservancy.

But it will be the showcase for the most high-end Mercedes models, such as the $350,000 Maybach. Mass-market cars meanwhile will be displayed in a new, adjoining showroom. Says Ralph S. Fischer, the dealership's general manager: "I mean, Frank Lloyd Wright design…That adds some mystique to the space and the design of our product."

For pictures, go to: www.galinsky.com/buildings/hoffman

Selfridges' Birmingham. (12/4/03). It has a reputation as a "rustbelt cripple," inhabited by "ruthlessly ironic, laconic and inherently nonchauvenistic" people, reports Warren Hodge in a *New York Times* article about Britain's second-largest city, Birmingham. Its "downtown tangle of freeways" is such a mess it's known as "Spaghetti Junction," and it has more lanes leaving the city than entering it.

Even Prince Charles piles on when it comes to Birmingham. He says its downtown area has "no charm, no human scale, no character except arrogance." Takes one to know one? (sorry).

But all of that is changing now in Birmingham, and it's all because of a *retailer*. Selfridges, selfridgesbirmingham.com, has transformed "an old market area known as the Bull Ring," www.bullring.co.uk, by erecting a $65 million building, a "curvy, undulating structure with a glittering surface of 15,000 reflective aluminum discs on a sheer cobalt blue skin." It is "astonishing," according to the critics back in London, and "could do for Birmingham what Frank Gehry's Guggenheim museum did for Bilbao in Spain."

The thing is, the Selfridges store, designed by a London firm called Future Systems, www.Future-Systems.com, is doing more than just adding a little razzle-dazzle to Birmingham's "reputation for strangling life and commerce in a collar of brutalist concrete."

The Selfridges sensation is now drawing attention to the city's parks—of which it has more than any other city in Britain. It has "more canals than Venice," too, which are no longer "filled with rusting bicycles" or providing escape routes for street criminals. Suddenly, people are noticing the "walkways and plazas" built over the past decade, the new Symphony Hall and the Balti Triangle, "a largely Pakistani area" with "more than 70 restaurants."

Even a *Times of London* critic, Lucia van der Post, has to admit it's all pretty impressive. "All in all," she writes of the Selfridges store, "it makes a trip to Birmingham seem like the must-have treat of the year."

Fashion & Art. (9/30/03). "Since Andy Warhol, expectations about the artist and the marketplace have changed rapidly," says Lisa Phillips of the New Museum, as quoted by Ruth La Ferla in *The New York Times* "In a post-Warholian world," she adds, "all of it flies." In her case, it flies as a Fendi-sponsored museum benefit that she hopes will also "court a broader public." She elaborates: "The audience for any kind of crossover activity is wider, but fashion is certainly something more people relate to as being a part of their daily lives."

Such thinking is not limited to museums, of course. High-end retailers increasingly are turning to fine artists "as the latest antidote to widespread consumer fatigue." Robert Burke of Bergdorf Goodman comments: "Store openings are a dime a dozen. A hard sell for clothing is stale. Customers no longer come in just to see new clothes."

For Mont Blanc, the notion manifests itself in the commissioning of "10 artists…to embellish 10-foot-high shopping bag sculptures, which will be displayed in Rockefeller Center next month to mark the opening of a new Manhattan store." The concept is meant to convey that "shopping is a higher art form," as explained by Jan-Patrick Schmitz, Montblanc's ceo.

Lord & Taylor's Fifth Avenue windows, meanwhile, are showcasing "the raucously comical canvases of the artist Red Grooms" alongside "a series of scarlet evening dresses. Elsewhere on Fifth Avenue, Ferragamo's features an art installation, as does the Giorgio Armani boutique at Bergdorf Goodman's, which also involves a charity tie-in.

All of this useful beauty works for the artists, to be sure. "It's awesome for an artist to be connected with fashion," says Amanda Church, an artist who added her artistic touch to a new Fendi handbag. "Besides," she says, "fashion has a lot of allure and glamour, something I think the art world hasn't quite achieved."

www.reveries.com

0-595-30641-1

Printed in the United States
18642LVS00007B/63